HISTORY TOURS OF TORQUAY

Philip Badcott

Copyright © 2021 Philip Badcott
All rights reserved
Cover photo by Philip Badcott
Maps by Philip Badcott
All rights reserved. No part of this book may be reproduced in any form or by written, electronic or mechanical, including photocopying, recording, or by any information retrieval system without written permission of the author.

Published by the author.

Although every precaution has been taken in the preparation of this book, the publisher and author assume no responsibility for errors or omissions. Neither is any liability assumed for damages resulting from the use of information contained herein.

ISBN: 9798733866703

FORWARD

There are already many books about the history of Torquay, and several about the various parishes in the town. The most comprehensive is Arthur Ellis's 'An Historical Survey of Torquay' published in 1930, whilst Leslie Lownds Pateman's 1991 Pictorial and Historical Survey of Babbacombe and St Marychurch Volume II is a mine of information about those two suburbs of the town. There are also several books written in the last 15 to 20 years about 20th-century Torquay. All have added to the body of knowledge of the town and are to be commended.

So why another history book about Torquay? In March 2020, just before the COVID-19 pandemic lockdown, I was invited by the President of the Torquay Museum Society to research the history behind some of Torquay Museum's magic lantern slides and then to present my findings at a Society lecture. However, due to the lockdown and the social distancing rules the lecture could not take place as planned. It was clear to me though that each of the 19 magic lantern slides researched had a much greater story than could be told in a few minutes at a lecture. I therefore decided to research the history behind some of the slides in greater depth. For example, the slide of Abbey Crescent on Torquay seafront has a history as interesting as any of the Regency-style buildings. The slide of the old bridge at Upton over Torquay's River Fleete was the catalyst that revealed the secrets of this now almost forgotten watercourse. Hence the more detailed studies of some of the slides became the chapters of this book and each chapter is a history tour of at least one part of Torquay. Being a Torquinian and a descendant of several long-established Torquay families, I have also made reference to some of my family by name and included the names of many others who lived in Torquay. Their history is part of the town and their stories may be of interest to family historians.

Many people have helped me with this book and my sincere thanks are extended to David Biggs, Heather Cooper, Carole Cresswell, Sue Harwood, Alan and Joan Henshaw, Cliff and Christine Howle, Colin and Vivienne King, Terry Leaman, Colin Roulstone, Leo Trewin, Tim Trewin and John Watt for providing information, memories and photos. Thanks also to Rowena Coote and Alan Henshaw for carefully reading my drafts and suggesting amendments. Those mentioned and others have supported and encouraged me in my endeavours. I am grateful also to Torquay Museum, the Torquay Museum Society and the South West Heritage Centre who have kindly allowed access to their pictorial archives and libraries that have been a rich source of information. Images that are not attributed are from the author's collection.

Philip Badcott (April 2021)

CONTENTS

	Page
A tour of Torquay using the Torquay Museum's magic lantern slides	1
An excursion to Abbey Crescent, the promenade and seafront	22
A visit to Meadfoot and Daddyhole Plain	44
A day out in the 19th century parish of St Marychurch	66
Following Torquay's River Fleete	103
A walk around Torquay Harbour	121
References	145
Index	147

CHAPTER 1

A TOUR OF TORQUAY USING THE TORQUAY MUSEUM'S MAGIC LANTERN SLIDES

Torquay Museum has several thousand magic lantern slides which have been digitised thanks to a National Lottery Heritage Grant. I was invited to research the history behind some of the slides and having done so, I then decided to make a tour of 19th-century Torquay starting and finishing at the museum using some of its wonderful slides.

From the museum we will walk down to the harbour, along the promenade and seafront to Torre Abbey and on to Cockington. Then we will visit Chelston, Upton, Watcombe, Kent's Cavern, Meadfoot and back to our starting point at the museum.

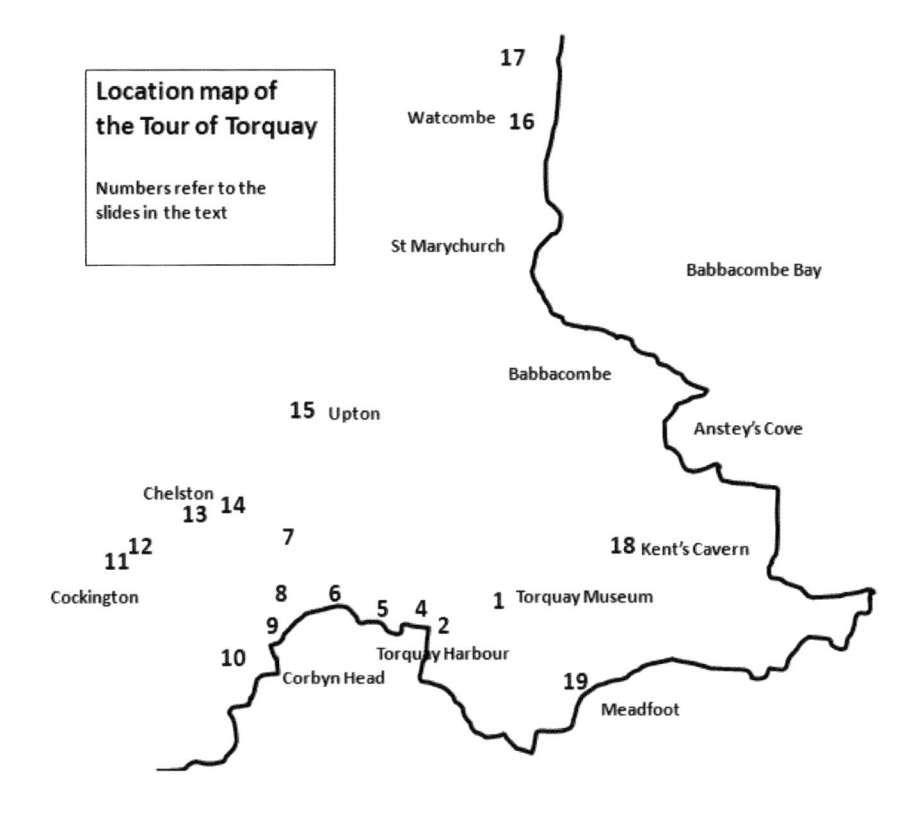

1

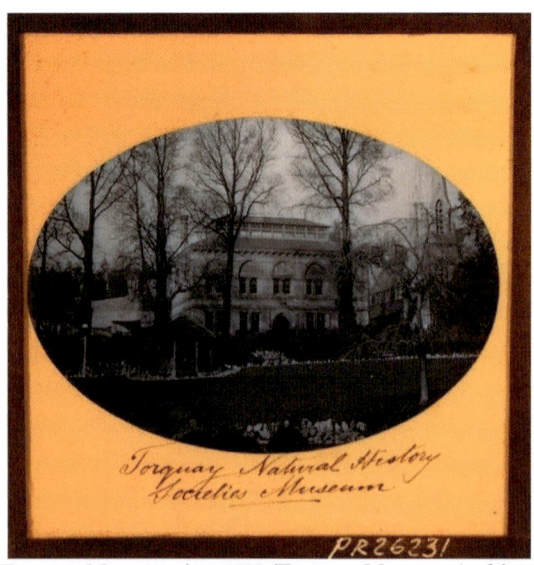

Slide 1 – Torquay Museum circa 1880 (Torquay Museum Archive PR26231)

    Here we are outside Torquay Museum in Babbacombe Road and the slide is labelled 'Torquay Natural History Societies Museum'. The shot was taken circa 1880 from across the road in Torwood Gardens. The octagonal shelter in the gardens is no longer there, but that seat to the left still exists.

    Next to the museum is the old Wesleyan Church, with its 140 foot spire built in 1873 mainly for visitors to the town. The location of the museum and church was described by Clayton Walker in 1904 as 'beautiful in situation, on a tree lined road with its fine residential mansions and in quite a fashionable part of the town'.

    The Torquay Natural History Society was formed in 1844 and had met in various places in the town. Then, in 1876, this purpose built museum was opened to display and store its huge collection. It is now Grade II listed and described as a 'Ruskinian Venetian Gothic' style building.

    An external feature is the arched brick recesses above the first floor windows. Two of the recesses, the first and third, are filled with terracotta relief panels of Torquay clay: one shows 'botany' and the other shows 'natural history'. The other three recesses were never filled, owing to a lack of funds. The museum is the home of Britain's oldest human – or rather its jawbone that was discovered at Kent's Cavern and it has been dated as 40,000 years old. The museum also has its amazing Devon Marble exhibition, the reconstructed Devon Farmhouse and a permanent Agatha Christie Exhibition. We will now walk down Babbacombe Road and Torwood Street to the Strand and the Queen's Family Hotel.

Slide 2 – Reading the Charter in 1892 (Torquay Museum Archive PR 26272)

Whatever is going on in Slide 2 at the Queen's Family Hotel situated on the Strand very near to the Mallock Clock Tower? It's the building that was renamed the Queen's Hotel, restyled into an art-deco building and is now called Queens Quay. But why are there so many people, why are the letters V and R displayed in the second floor windows and why are the flags flying? Could it be Queen Victoria's Golden Jubilee in 1887? Surprisingly it's not. The date is 1 September 1892 and it's the reading and celebration of the Charter of Incorporation of Torquay Borough Council.

The Charter was signed by Her Majesty Queen Victoria on 12 August 1892 and it was brought by a special train from London on 1 September. Then, a procession that was nearly a mile long marched from Torquay Station along the seafront, up Belgrave Road to Brunswick Square and then down South Street, Union Street and Fleet Street to the Strand. It included the Volunteer Artillery, a tableaux depicting the harbour and the gardens of Torquay, the High Sheriff of Devon attended by heralds, the Tormohun Hussars, the Lifeboat and its crew, and 2,500 children each wearing a medal to commemorate the day. After a fanfare by the Heralds, the Charter was read from the balcony of the Queen's Family Hotel by the Mayor to 10,000 people. By 1900, St Marychurch, Babbacombe, Cockington and Chelston had become part of the Borough. The success of Torquay as a town in the 20th century had been secured. On the right hand side of the hotel is a two-storey building. It is the last remaining house from the 1810 terrace that once stretched the length of Victoria Parade making it one of the oldest buildings in the harbour area.

Slide 3 – Torquay's first Mayor in 1892 (Torquay Museum Archive PR26271)

William Francis Splatt was elected as Torquay's first mayor on 9 November 1892. It was he who read the Charter from the Queen's Family Hotel and had the privilege of being one of the five dignitaries who brought the Charter from London.

William Splatt was a Devonian and was born in Chudleigh in 1811, seven years before my great-great grandfather John Badcock was born in the same town. But whereas my ancestor made his way to Torquay in 1841 in a straightforward way via Newton Abbot, William Splatt did it the hard way.

In 1841 he sailed to Australia where he became a member of the first Legislative Council of the State of Victoria. He became very wealthy after successful banking and farming ventures and returned to England in 1854. He eventually settled in Torquay in 1876 in a house and estate called The Elms in Torre which was situated on what became the Torquay Boys' Grammar School and then the South Devon College Campus. It is now the Torre Marine housing estate.

Councillor William Splatt had the honour of being presented with Torquay's mayoral chain in January 1893, but he died suddenly in October that year aged 82. By 1930 a portrait of him was hung in Torquay Town Hall. Hoping that the crowds have dispersed we will now stand outside the Queen's Family Hotel and look across to what was once a derelict building site.

Slide 4 - Outside the Royal Hotel 1892 (Torquay Museum Archive PR26232)

Slide 4 is an 1892 image of a horse-drawn carriage that might have provided a bus service between Torquay Station and St Marychurch. It is parked on the Strand by the Queen Victoria Jubilee Street Lamp which was erected in 1887, but removed in 1902 when the Mallock Clock Tower was built on the same spot. Thankfully the lamp standard was not destroyed and sits in the St Marychurch Precinct adjacent to the Dolphin Inn.

The building that was demolished was part of the Royal Hotel and replaced in circa 1900 by the interesting terracotta brick building that was first an upholsterers and more recently a pizza restaurant.

The Royal Hotel, formally The London Inn, dates from 1774 and was the first hotel and coach house in Torquay. By 1822 it had a grand ballroom designed by John Foulston and described by an Exeter newspaper as 'the most splendid building of the sort of any watering place in the West of England'. The sizeable hotel included the properties either side of this building plot.

Some distance behind is Higher Terrace built in 1811 as apartments for visitors and incomers who were flocking to the town. It is now one of Torquay's oldest buildings. When I was a boy my dentist, Mr Barnes, had his consulting room overlooking the harbour, so this view brings back memories of laughing gas and the words 'open wide!' My parents always called Higher Terrace 'The White House' and in Number 1 The White House there was for a while a solicitor's office called Perry Mason.

Slide 5 - Torbay Hotel 1892 (Torquay Museum Archive PR26269)

Here is another 1892 slide and this one is of the Exeter stagecoach outside the Torbay Hotel that overlooks the Princess Gardens and I think the carriage has the word KENTON of the side. Kenton is a village on the Exe Estuary road between Starcross and Exminster. Presumably there was a change of horses there after passing through St Marychurch, Shaldon, Teignmouth and Dawlish. Even in 1892 the stagecoach was still in competition with the railways that came to Torquay in 1848.

The Torbay Hotel is also one of Torquay's earliest and the ornate pillars still exist although the verandah behind has been enclosed to enlarge the interior of the hotel. To the left hand side of this slide a terrace of five very large and elegant houses was built in 1854 called Sulyarde Terrace that became a hotel called Cumper's Hotel in 1859. To the right hand side of the Cumper's Hotel, the Torbay Hotel was built a little later in 1866. The two amalgamated in 1902 and the gap between the two hotels was in-filled with what is now the main entrance. A feature in the hotels was the suites that were named after Devon Sea Dogs: Sir Walter Raleigh, Sir Francis Drake, John Hawkins and … Sir Martin Frobisher. Except that he was a Yorkshireman! The hotel was and maybe still is in a precarious position being in front of Waldon Hill also known as Rock Walk.

In the second half of the 19th century there were some huge rock falls at the back of the hotel. If you do stay at the Torbay Hotel, ask for a room at the front overlooking Princess Gardens. At the time of writing, the hotel is closed owing to the COVID-19 pandemic lockdown and there are fears that it may not reopen.

Slide 6 - Abbey Crescent 1893 (Torquay Museum Archive PR26260)

We are now at the other end of the promenade and approaching Abbey Crescent which was built in 1858 as a terrace of 10 elegant Regency-style houses. The builders of Abbey Crescent disposed of the excess soil in an ingenious way. A tramway was constructed from the building site to Torre Abbey Meadows and the soil taken by trolleys and dumped.

By 1893 when this image was taken little had changed but during the 20th century the crescent was extended upwards and became the upmarket Palm Court Hotel. In the 1980s and 1990s it gradually went downhill, becoming a café/bar. Then in 2010 it was ravaged and destroyed by fire. From its ashes rose the new Abbey Crescent of homes, holiday apartments and restaurants. Is the new building, I ask myself, worthy of the name? However, the last two houses of the original crescent on the right hand side were not affected by the fire and in 2021 Number 1 Abbey Crescent is a restaurant and Number 2 a fish and chip café.

The Old Toll House is to the right of the crescent. It was erected to serve the new Torquay to Paignton road that was built in 1842. At the time of this slide it was the home of the town's gardener and called Rock Cottage. It has also served as the beach manager's office, public toilets and is now waiting to be transformed into perhaps, a 21st-century café. In 1934 significant land reclamation permitted the road and pavements to be widened and the sunken gardens to be built that now run along the promenade to the Princess Theatre. This immediately became a very attractive asset to the seafront area.

Slide 7 - Lime Avenue 1859 (Torquay Museum Archive PR26229)

Our next location is an atmospheric road in the old Torre Abbey Estate of snow-covered Lime Avenue that tells us quite a lot about the history of Torre Abbey. In the 19th century Torre Abbey had as well as its garden a park called 'Torabbey Park'. This unusual spelling is used in the 1869 OS map. The park was substantial with its western border extending from the sea up King's Drive and Avenue Road to the junction with Old Mill Road, and then up Mill Lane to the Lych Gate of the old Torre Church, and then down Sands Lane that became Belgrave Road to the sea.

There were three private drives to Torre Abbey called Chestnut Avenue, Elm Avenue and Long Avenue. Chestnut Avenue is the road from Belgrave Road leading to the English Riviera Centre and Abbey Gates. Elm Avenue consisted of a double row of elm trees on one side of the road and a row of lime trees on the other side and was renamed Avenue Road. Then there was Long Avenue that stretched from Abbey Gates up to Belgrave Road and in the second half of the 19th century the lower section was renamed Falkland Avenue and then Falkland Road. The top 150 yards of Long Avenue became Lime Avenue and still exists and is now a residential street where sadly only three lime trees remain. Nevertheless, Lime Avenue was once one part of the Torre Abbey's private drives. But is this slide Lime Avenue? I think not because the road is too long. I think this is Elm Avenue with its rows of Elms and Limes. Over time, the Carys of Torre Abbey sold off sections of the park to make way for the building of villas and hotels. Opposite Falkland Road is Lucius Street and both are named after Sir Lucius Cary, 2nd Viscount Falkland the most famous Cary of all the Torre Abbey Cary family. He died in the Civil War aged 34.

Slide 8 – Spanish Barn in 1860 (Torquay Museum Archive PR26282)

We are now outside the Spanish Barn in the grounds of Torre Abbey in 1860, or to give it its old name, the Tithe Barn. It was part of the Premonstratensian Torre Abbey founded in 1196 to hold their substantial grain harvests from their considerable lands and the tithes due to them by tenant farmers. However, in the 14th century, the Abbot himself owed his own tithe due to the king. Geoffrey Gilbert of Compton Castle who was the local tax collector was instructed to visit the Abbot to demand payment.

The Spanish Barn is best known for holding 397 Spanish sailors and soldiers as prisoners from the 'Nostra Senora del Rosario' at the time of the Spanish Armada in 1588. The ship had been captured by Sir Francis Drake, handed over to Sir Walter Raleigh's ship the 'Roebuck' which brought it to Tor Bay. The prisoners were handed over to Sir George Cary of Cockington, and to Sir John Gilbert of Greenway. However, much to the annoyance of George Cary, Sir John Gilbert took advantage and put 106 prisoners to work on his estate at Greenway to level the grounds. I think George Cary wished he had thought of the idea first. Then Sir John Gilbert also wanted all the wine on board the Rosario for himself - and this too annoyed George Cary. It is said that he sulked for years.

By the 1900s the ivy had been removed from the barn and it was in a slightly better condition than in 1860. Then, in 1930 Torre Abbey along with the Spanish Barn were sold by the Cary family to Torquay Council and restored into the fine building we have today.

Slide 9 – The storm of 1859 (Torquay Museum Archive PR35674)

This is the sea wall opposite King's Drive after the gale of the 25th and 26th October 1859. At the time it was unequalled in living memory for its widespread destruction across the South West. Imagine standing high up in Rock Walk overlooking the promenade. You would see 20-foot rollers as far as the eye could see advancing towards the shore. By the Torbay Hotel, the nearby Princess Gardens had yet to be created and the sea came right up to the coast road outside the hotel and 30 yards of the road disappeared.

However, Abbey Crescent was unscathed but a hundred yards farther along the coast road at the bottom of Belgrave Road massive 7 ton blocks of sandstone were carried from the sea wall across the road. A long stretch of the sea wall was breached and the wooden Toll House that had replaced the Old Toll House was washed up on Torre Abbey Meadows towards the Spanish Barn. The meadows themselves were under 6 feet of water and the Spanish Barn had huge waves reaching and crashing into it. There was also destruction around the harbour, the Strand, at Livermead and Meadfoot.

The steep slope at the top right of the slide is Sheddon Hill and to the right of it is the small triangular plot of land now called Old Maid's Perch. It was given to the town in 1866 by R S S Cary of Torre Abbey and had been a favourite spot for visitors and locals alike to sit and enjoy the view.

Unfortunately in 2012 Torbay Council authorised the sale of 83 square metres of Old Maid's Perch to the new owners of the Palm Court Hotel. Six benches that had the best views of the bay have been lost and much of Old Maid's Perch is no more. The sold plot is now used as a restaurant terrace which blocks out the sea view from the few remaining public seats that are behind it.

Slide 10 – Corbyn Head 1858 (Torquay Museum Archive PR26243)

A few minutes' walk from the breached sea wall is Corbyn Head and in 1858 it was the home of the guns of the Artillery Volunteers. In the 1850s there was concern that France might stage an invasion under Napoleon III. The threat was real because with the advent of steamships an invasion journey across the Channel from Cherbourg would take just seven hours.

In 1853 the Torquay Volunteer Company was formed and then in December 1859, the Fourth Devon Volunteer Artillery Battery was formed by Edward Vivian who became its Major. On 4 May 1860 the government supplied it with two 24-pounder guns that were placed on Corbyn Head. The date on the slide of 1858 might be incorrect and could be 1860 or later. Major Vivian is sat on Corbyn Head with two ladies relaxing and admiring the view. There are no railings along the cliff edge and few buildings above the harbour.

It's fitting that the Artillery Volunteers - the Home Guard of the 1850s – have their guns on this spot because Corbyn Head is now the home of the National Home Guard Memorial. Unveiled in 2005 it remembers the 1,206 Home Guards killed in World War II, including the nine killed at Corbyn Head, the Barton Gas Works and the Palace Hotel.

Edward Vivian was a pillar of Torquay Society. He was born in 1809 and a founder of the Torquay Natural History Society and business partner and editor of the Torquay Directory Newspaper. He wrote under the signature 'Censor' and it is said that he often altered the content of letters sent to the newspaper before publication to tone down or up as he thought appropriate.

Slide 11 – Cockington Ducking Stool (Torquay Museum Archive PR26276)

From Corbyn Head we've made our way further along Torbay Road and turned up Cockington Lane, walked through the meadow, then on to the road again and arrived at Cockington Forge and the Rose Cottage Tea Rooms. And here is a sketch of the ducking stool and forge at this very spot in Cockington. The forge is thought to date back to the 14th century, is Grade II listed and for centuries it was supported on three wooden posts, but Historic England and/or Torbay Council have allowed a fourth post to be erected which, in my opinion, should not have been authorised.

In the Middle Ages the Lord of the Manor had the power and administration of capital punishment. At Cockington he had a pool to drown the women, and even today there is a small lake in grounds of Rose Cottage at the spot of the old ducking pool.

There was also a whipping post and stocks nearby. The gallows to hang the men were at Gallows Gate, at the top of Shiphay by the ancient ridgeway where the four parishes of Cockington, Marldon, St Marychurch and Kingskerswell met.

I remember as a boy sitting in the old stocks at Cockington pretending to have rotten fruit and vegetables thrown at me. But where are these stocks now? The only stocks in the village are a new pair in the Rose Tea Garden. Thankfully there are still ancient stocks on display in Torquay Museum's Devon Farmhouse exhibition.

Slide 12 – Court Cottage (Torquay Museum Archive PR36314)

This is Court Cottage, also known as the Old Schoolhouse and is a 16th-century farmhouse in Cockington. It's in Cockington Square on the opposite side of Vicarage Hill to the Rose Tea Gardens. It is now a gift shop and has hidden beneath its floorboards an ancient cobbled floor.

The writing on the left-hand side of the slide says: 'Old Cockington Village. The Crosses Dairies'. Along the right-hand side it reads. 'School 1870, Mrs Doney, window put in the end of the room as now. Estate Office 1808'. The building was the Cockington School between 1862 and 1892 and was run by Mrs Suzannah Doney for her five children and the children of the village. She was paid 2d a week by the poor parents and 6d from the better off. She continued as the school teacher until 1892 when the school relocated to a new purpose-built school in Old Mill Road.

The bottom edge of the slide reads: 'Mr Cross' and 'Old Well'. There is a John Cross in the 1861 census aged 58. He was an agricultural labourer so the person in the slide could be him or a relative who has used or just about to use the horse plough. There is now no trace of the well on the right hand side of the gate. One theory is that the stream flowing down from Cockington Park via Flower's Watermill may have fed this well but was diverted at some time.

Court Cottage may also have been Court House but there is no actual evidence of this, but it is near to the Ducking Stool.

Slide 13 – **Pomery Bridge over Sherwell Stream (Torquay Museum Archive PR35716)**

We are now in Lower Chelston at the stone-built Pomery Bridge over the Sherwell Stream. It was situated in Old Mill Road and opposite the current Cockington School. Its source was the three springs at the top of Sherwell Valley Road that are now buried under Sherwell Valley School. The stream was extremely important over the centuries as a source of drinking water. It fed three ponds near its source and also powered the old mill that we will discuss on the next slide. The scene here in circa 1860 is, of course, totally unrecognisable today. The gentle hill on the far side of the bridge is Old Mill Road that now has its terraces of shops on either side.

After flowing under Pomery Bridge the Sherwell Stream ran parallel with today's Rosery Road although its natural course was diverted by the cutting of the railway in 1847. It then joined up with the Fullford Brook also known as Chapel Hill Stream near Torre Abbey. At Abbey Gates the Fullford Brook divided into two. One stream fed two fishponds on Torre Abbey Meadows and the Torre Abbey waterwheel. The other stream flowed towards the vicinity of the grandly named King's Gardens and fed a pool called the 'fleet's watering place' where His Majesty's ships and others replenished their water supplies in the 19th century.

Today the stream feeds the two lakes in King's Gardens where in springtime the ducks and swans nest and nurture their young. A 21st-century legend is that two eccentric gentlemen who live nearby consider themselves as the swans' midwives. It takes all sorts I suppose. The Sherwell stream ends its 1.6 mile journey by entering the sea on the eastern side of Corbyn Beach.

Slide 14 – The old mill at Chelston (Torquay Museum Archive PR35707)

Here is a slide taken in 1860 of the old mill at Chelston powered by the Sherwell Stream. At first glance the location of this waterwheel is obvious. It's in Chelston and there was definitely a mill that was powered by the Sherwell Stream and located near to Pomery Bridge. It was called Herring's Mill and was demolished in 1878. However this image is different from another in the reliable reference book 'Cockington Bygones'. So where is this mill?

There was and still is a waterwheel at Cockington near the Drum Inn called Flower's Watermill and most South Devon people are familiar with it. It sits firmly against a sturdy stone building rather than this part-stone and part-wooden structure and it's probably a larger wheel than this one. This magic lantern slide is definitely not it!

Another mill was at the junction of Old Mill Road and Cockington Lane by the gate to the Cockington water meadows. It was fed by a leat that drew water from the stream running through the water meadows. This time an old sketch purporting to be that mill is different from the magic lantern slide. I have to admit that I'm flummoxed. It is certainly a ruin and must, by the look of it, have been one for some time. It's time to move to another slide and another part of Torquay.

Slide 15 – The old bridge at Upton (Torquay Museum Archive PR26230)

    We have now walked about half a mile from Old Mill Road to the suburb of Upton to look for the bridge in slide 15. On the side of this slide are the words: 'The Old Bridge at Upton – Torquay'. So where exactly is it? My first thoughts were that it was on Penny's Hill, just before the junction with Lymington Road with a view of the thatched Penny's Cottage and Daison Hill. But it can't be because there is no river to cross up from Penny's Cottage.

    Further research was needed. There were three old bridges in Upton that crossed the River Fleete. The River Fleete itself is more like a stream and has its source in Watcombe. From there it flows under Teignmouth Road, Lymington Road, Union Street and Fleet Walk to enter the sea at Torquay Harbour. The three bridges in Upton were these: one at the bottom of Wright's Lane not far from Penny's Cottage, another at the bottom of Chatto Road and the third one at what is now the corner of Upton Road and Lymington Road.

    One thing to bear in mind is that Lymington Road and the terraces of houses either side of it were not built until the end of the 19th century. The scene and the road layout at the time of this slide were completely different from today's. The gentleman in the picture is heading towards the cluster of cottages in old Upton and a limestone quarry beyond. The only bridge that would have had this view was the bridge at the corner of Upton Road and Lymington Road and the character in the slide is facing the old quarry in St James Road.

Slide 16 – Giant Rock Watcombe 1862 (Torquay Museum Archive PR26259)

From Upton we head out along Lymington Road and Teignmouth Road to Watcombe when we turn right at the sign for Watcombe Beach. From Watcombe Beach car park we walk 30 yards along the coast path and look up. Through the trees you will see this 150 foot high Giant Rock of sandstone conglomerate. It's in the Valley of the Rocks on the coast path between Watcombe Beach and Maidencombe. Until the end of the 19th century the area was grazed and treeless like the scene in this slide. When grazing stopped, the area reverted to its natural woodland state. So that's why the scene in the slide is almost unrecognizable as Watcombe. In the distance is the Goats' Path leading eventually to Maidencombe.

Below the Giant Rock is what 'The Torquay Directory' newspaper described as a natural amphitheatre formed in remote ages by a gigantic landslip and called the Valley of the Rocks where, on 1 September 1853, an extraordinary event took place. It was the 'musical fete champetre' organised by the Torquay Choral Society – a garden party on a huge scale. 8,000 people attended including those who came by train from Birmingham and London and were then ferried from Torquay Harbour to Watcombe Beach by steamer. The band of the Royal Marines and the Torquay Subscription band stood below the Giant Rock playing away. A 100-strong choir sang, children danced around a maypole and cream teas were served. There were however downsides to the fete. There was the daunting task of organising toilet facilities for 8,000 people in an out-of-the-way place. But the biggest concern was that only one-third paid for admission to the fete, with even many of the well-dressed avoiding payment. The musical fete champetre was never held again.

Slide 17 – **Torquay tradesmen's outing in August 1861 (Torquay Museum Archive PR26273)**

Here we have forty or so tradesmen enjoying their annual outing in 1861. The slide does not tell us where it is, but I'm assuming that it is not far from Torquay, and might just be a half-day's outing. My best guess is that it's between Watcombe and Maidencombe and maybe the tradesmen are looking out to sea.

A dozen or so are wearing their three-piece suits and top hats even in August. Others appear to be in lighter-coloured clothes and some are not quite so smartly dressed.

Tradesmen in the 19th century were those who had had specialised training to do their work. Some produced and sold goods from their own premises. Examples are boot makers, potters, saddlers, cabinet makers and stonemasons. They might employ other skilled workers and factory hands too. I'm wondering if one of them is a local stonemason Richard Moxhay. Sir Edmund Gosse, the writer and critic, and son of the marine biologist Philip Gosse grew up in St Marychurch in the 1850s and 1860s and he describes Richard Moxhay in his book 'Father and Son':

> *'He was always dressed in a white corduroy suit and any stain of Devonshire mud was painfully conspicuous. When smartened up, his appearance suggested that somebody had given a coating of whitewash which looked like Devonshire cream.'*

The outing must have been a welcome break to these men who through their skills and hard work facilitated the growth of Torquay in the 19th century. The population grew from 831 in 1801 to 16,417 in 1861.

Slide 18 – Kent's Cavern (Torquay Museum Archive PR36367)

We've made our way back via St Marychurch and Babbacombe to the famous Kent's Cavern in Ilsham Road. And it was the home of Britain's oldest human and his or her jawbone was discovered in 1927 by Arthur Ogilvie, the curator of Torquay Museum. It is now on display at the museum and has been dated as 40,000 years old.

The first detailed exploration of Kent's Cavern was in 1827 by Father John MacEnery, the chaplain of Torre Abbey, during his summer retreat at nearby Ilsham Chapel. He uncovered the bones of extinct prehistoric animals and man-made flint tools. His explorations inspired William Pengelly to make his own systematic explorations at both Kent's Cavern and Windmill Hill Cave in Brixham between 1865 and 1880. The cave in the slide is the one that has the stalagmite which one can touch and make a wish, but not tell anyone what your wish is or it won't come true.

And do you know how Kent's Cavern got its name? Back in the distant past, a dog was at the entrance to the cave and some Devon pixies teased it by pulling the hair off its back. The dog was terrified and ran into the cave, and kept running and running as a three-line rhyme tells us:

> An 'ee went, an 'ee went.
> Until he comed out.
> In the County of Kent.

Hence the name Kent's Cavern. The caves were bought by Francis Powe in 1903 from Sir Lawrence H Palk also known as Lord Haldon. The cavern is still in 2021 owned by the Powe family.

Slide 19 – Hesketh Crescent (Torquay Museum Archive PR35654)

From Kent's Cavern it's a twenty-minute walk along Ilsham Green and Meadfoot Sea Road to the magnificent Hesketh Crescent that sits above Meadfoot Beach. It was commissioned by Lawrence V Palk and built in 1848 by the builders J T and W Harvey. At the time it was said that: 'the proportions are perfect and the quality of the ornamental stone and ironwork places the building in a class of its own'. Another commentator remarked that it was: 'the finest crescent of houses in the West of England' and an 1851 visitor Sir James Morrison tells us that it is: 'adapted for the higher class of company'. We might know the building as the Osborne Hotel which dates from 1853 and today the crescent is mix of private apartments, holiday apartments, and a hotel. However, it is still well worth wandering along the outside to grasp the sheer scale and beauty of the building.

The slide is a view from Daddy Hole Plain which in the 1850s was known as Daddy's Hole and previously had the name Devil's Hole - the place of the Legend of Torquay and The Demon Hunter. The scene unlike today is a treeless coastline and not one other house is in the vicinity. This suggests that it is one of the earliest pictures of Hesketh Crescent. A later 1867 picture has several houses above it and in the distance, Kilmorie House. The slide also shows Orestone and Thatcher Rock with the smaller Shag Rock out of shot. Sir James calls these: 'the three island rocks which form interesting objects' and they certainly do enhance the glorious view out to sea.

Our tour of Torquay is almost at an end. All we need to do now is make our way back to the museum. I suggest via the scenic coast path and the harbour.

Dedication

This 'Tour of Torquay' is dedicated to my late brother Trevor Badcott (1945-2020). He was Torquay's Magic Lantern man. Around 1980 Trevor acquired from our father his Victorian Magic Lantern and its 2,000 slides. Since then Trevor presented many dozens of slide shows including his now well-known 'Tour of South Devon', a cartoon slide show and the story of the Devon Regiment in the Boer War. In doing so he raised hundreds of pounds for Rowcroft Hospice. And no one can be more Devonian and Torquinian than Trevor because he lived in Torquay all his life.

Trevor's life was a life of service in so many spheres. He was an extremely practical man and could turn his hand to almost anything and used his skills to maintain and improve the buildings at Upton Vale Baptist Church, Central Church and more recently at St Andrew's Church in Shiphay. Another great love of Trevor's was playing the tuba with Bay Brass which he did for over twenty years.

Trevor Badcott and his Victorian Magic Lantern at Kingskerswell Library October 2019

CHAPTER 2

AN EXCURSION TO ABBEY CRESCENT, THE PROMENADE AND SEAFRONT

Imagine that you are on holiday in Torquay in 1855 and you're staying a mile from Torquay Harbour on the coast road at the Livermead House Hotel. On the first morning of your holiday, just before breakfast, you have a stroll towards Corbyn Beach and along the way you look across the bay towards Torquay Harbour and the expanding town.

You will no doubt see and admire the beautifully proportioned Higher Terrace built in 1811, the first St John's Church built in 1823 proudly overlooking the harbour and the harbour itself built in 1806 that was paid for by Sir Lawrence Palk the Lord of the Manor of Torre.

You'll spot Sulyarde Terrace gleaming in the morning sunlight that was built a year before your holiday and destined to become the Torbay Hotel, and the brand new villas on Waldon Hill above Rock Walk, then known as the Fishermen's Path will also catch your eye.

But you will not see another of Torquay's grand terraces of ten very nice houses. I'm talking about Abbey Crescent also known as The Palm Court Hotel that stood at the far end of Torre Abbey Sands, right on the bend in the road. Abbey Crescent wasn't built until 1858 and has an interesting story as any of Torquay's Regency-style buildings.

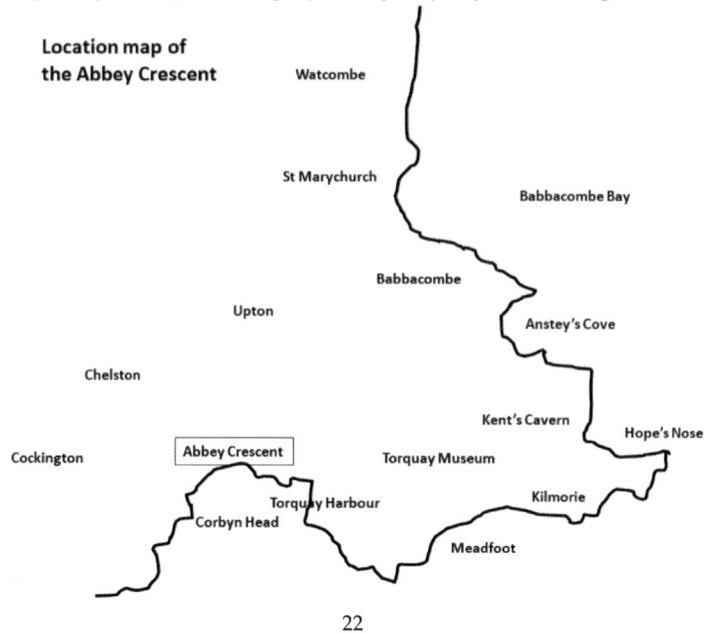

Location map of the Abbey Crescent

Figure 1 - Abbey Crescent built in 1858

Before 1842 there was no coast road from Torquay Harbour to Paignton, and hence there was no incentive or reason to build on the site of Abbey Crescent. To get to Paignton from Torquay Harbour before the coast road was built, one had to travel up narrow Swan Street, Abbey Road to Torre, through a farmyard behind Torre Abbey, then towards Cockington and up along the old Paignton Road no wider than a cart. The coast road in Figure 1 did not exist. Once built the new coast road did however transform travel between the two towns, in the same way that Kingskerswell bypass has transformed travel from Torquay and Paignton to Newton Abbot and beyond in the last few years. The coast road opened up the opportunity to build houses, villas and hotels.

In Figure 2, circa 1870, a few promenaders are sitting at the base of Old Maid's Perch, while a boy is playing with his hoop and stick. The horse and carriages might be taking their passengers to Torquay Railway Station or further afield to Paignton. The original toll house building in the picture still exists. It looks rather like a small chapel.

Abbey Crescent was built into the side of a steep shrubbery bank and in 1855 building preparations had commenced. Figure 3 is a sketch of the Torquay Volunteer Regiment on exercise at Torre Abbey Meadows on the 25 July 1855. In the forefront are the trees that have already been felled to make way for the crescent and the soldiers are running across what is today Sheddon Hill. There were two builders: Robert Henley constructed the west end of the crescent and John Harvey the east end. However, they must have used the same plans because the front of the building is symmetrical.

Figure 2 - The new coast road from Torquay Harbour to Paignton circa 1870
(Torquay Museum Society Library)

Figure 3 – Torre Abbey Meadows July 1855

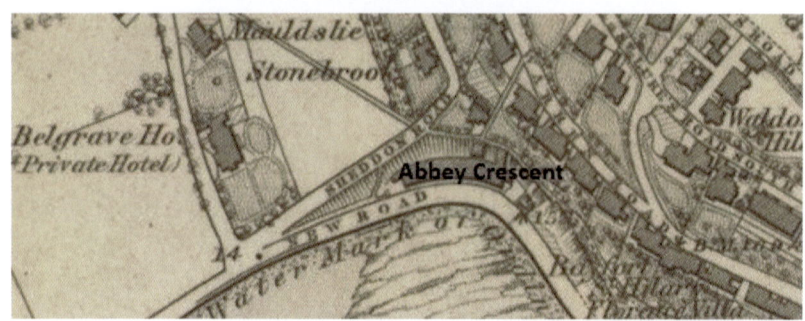

Figure 4 – OS Map surveyed 1863
(Reproduced with the permission of the National Library of Scotland)

The excess soil from the excavated bank was disposed of in an ingenious way. The builders laid a tramway from the site to Torre Abbey Meadows and the soil was taken by trolleys – most likely horse-drawn -

and dumped on the site of the miniature golf course that opened in 1923 in front of Abbey Gardens (Figure 10) and not surprisingly, a strong retaining wall at the rear of Abbey Crescent had to be constructed. At the front a low balustrade wall was erected to provide small frontages facing the road.

Abbey Crescent, a terrace of ten very attractive houses of different sizes, was completed in 1858. Number 1 (at the Old Toll House end) and Number 10 at the west end appear to be the largest, and Numbers 5 and 6 which are the two centre houses also appear particularly grand. Most have attic rooms with one window facing the front and no doubt one at the back.

The 1863 map in Figure 4 shows the sweep of Abbey Crescent in the bend of the coast road then called New Road. Behind the crescent are the steep back gardens that slope up to Sheddon Hill then called Sheddon Road. Also behind the crescent is the Fishermen's Path renamed Rock Walk with its stupendous views of Tor Bay.

The 1861 census certainly makes interesting reading. Within the ten houses there are twenty households and a total of 78 persons. That's an average of almost 8 per house. Seven houses had lodging house keepers, and all but one shared the house with one or more other households. I would imagine that these up-market lodging houses in Abbey Crescent were used by those who had moved to Torquay and were acquiring permanent homes as well as those holidaying in the town.

In Number 1, Emma Harvey was the head of her household and a lodging house keeper. She lived with her three children, a housemaid and a border who was a draper. Also in Number 1 lived Jessy Montague who was the head of her household. She was the widow of an officer in the British Army. Her son, Arthur, was born in Hobart, Van Diemen's Land.

In Number 9 lived George Dance as the only householder. He was aged 42 and his occupation was 'a clergyman without cure of souls', in other words, an unemployed vicar. He must have been comfortably well off as he had three servants to look after him, his wife and son.

Out of the 78 who lived in Abbey Crescent at the time of the 1861 census just 21 were born in South Devon. This is not surprising because large numbers of the comfortably well off flocked to the town in the 19th century to live in the elegant villas that were springing up. An 1851 visitor, Sir James Morrison, wrote: 'building going on rapidly and innumerable villas are raised tier upon tier to the summits of the hills, standing in their own beautiful grounds, or miniature paddocks'.

Many others moved to Torquay for work and lived in the terraces of Torre, Swan Street, George Street, Higher Union Street, Lower Union Street and Pimlico. In 1801 the population of the town was just 838 and in the decade from 1851 to 1861, the population of the town grew from 11,474 to 16,417. That's a staggering 43% increase in just ten years.

In 1866 R S S Cary of Torre Abbey leased to the town the small triangular plot between New Road and Sheddon Road (Figure 4) which was subsequently conveyed to the town. It was remodelled into a small garden and terrace and became known as Old Maid's Perch that has been a favourite sitting place for residents and visitors until 2015 when Torbay Council authorised its sale.

On 30 August 1870 the building of the slipway opposite Abbey Crescent commenced. This now gave easy access to the beach. Imagine living in Abbey Crescent and being able to cross the road and walk quickly and easily to the sandy shoreline. However, a huge problem was looming over the town that made Torre Abbey Sands a smelly and filthy place to walk along and a health hazard to swim from.

Prior to 1878 one of Torquay's three sewer outlets to the sea was opposite Belgrave Hotel, just a stone's throw from Abbey Crescent. Another was opposite King's Gardens near to Corbyn Head. Torre Abbey Sands and Corbyn Head Beach could not have been pleasant places to sit on or swim from. The third outlet was near the Pavilion just outside the Inner Harbour. The 1878 solution was a new sewage system. The outlets from King's Drive and Belgrave Road were piped behind Abbey Crescent through a tunnel in Waldon Hill to join the Pavilion outlet. All sewage then flowed via pipes and tunnels to the brand new Hope's Nose sewage outlet. I remember hurrying past its ventilation shaft tower at Hope's Nose when I was a boy when on my way to fish at Hope's Nose and the smell from the shaft was as one can imagine overpoweringly revolting. This sewage system was in use until 2002 when the Brokenbury treatment plant at Churston was opened and serves all of Torbay.

Before Princess Pier was built, there was a proposal in December 1881 to erect a pier opposite Abbey Crescent. This was never built but, had it been, the history of Torre Abbey Sands and Abbey Crescent would have been very different. It seems a strange idea because boats and ships would only have been able to moor close to the promenade at high tide.

The 1893 Magic Lantern Slide (Figure 5) shows that Abbey Crescent had changed little in its first 40 years. There are a variety of blinds at the windows and neat hedges at the front and side. The slide also shows a gas lamp on the pavement and ornate iron railings and pillars running along the sea wall. However, the road alongside Rock Walk is narrower than it is today and there is no sign yet of the sunken gardens that now run along the promenade to the Princess Theatre. That had to wait until 1933-1934 when significant land reclamation permitted the road to be widened and the sunken gardens to be built (Figure 26).

Figure 5 - Abbey Crescent in 1893 (Torquay Museum Archive PR 26260)

By 1905 (Figure 6) there was still little change to Abbey Crescent although the coast road had been renamed from New Road to Torbay Road. The limestone walls of Rock Walk high up and behind the crescent can be seen and there are a few people enjoying walking along the seafront. This is a sign of things to come.

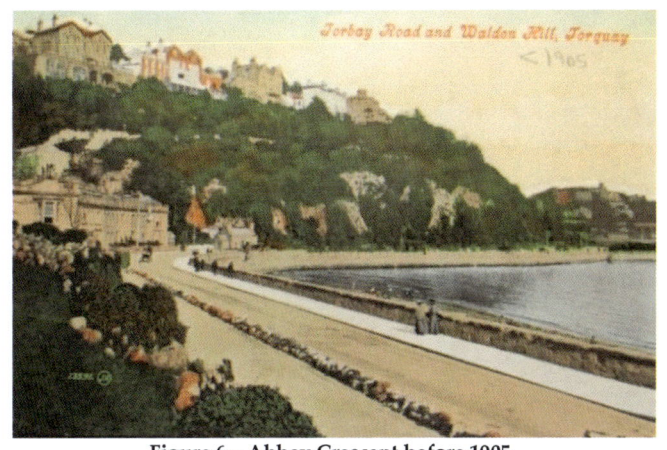

Figure 6 – Abbey Crescent before 1905

Figure 7 is another view of the unchanged Abbey Crescent in 1906. The 1870 slipway is visible with 20 or 30 people on the beach and the Old Maid's Perch has shrubs and greenery. Behind it is another of Torquay's early hotels. Built in 1859 Belgrave House was eventually named the Belgrave Hotel. It is still there serving customers 170 years later under the Premier Inn brand with the name Belgrave Sands Hotel and Spa.

R S S Cary of Torre Abbey had given the town the freehold of the slopes of Waldon Hill and the paths known as Rock Walk were laid in 1883, but it was not until 1893 that the wide path (Figure 7) or 'raised promenade' as it was known, was built. The path was named the 'Royal Terrace Gardens' whereas Torquinians just use the name Rock Walk.

Figure 7 – Abbey Crescent circa 1906 from Terrace Walk.

Figure 8 – Rock Walk and Old Toll House circa 1910

At the time of the 1901 census the occupancy of Abbey Crescent compared to the 1861 census was unchanged. There were 55 occupants in nine of the houses (the occupants of Number 7 were away on census day). There were 18 households compared to 20 in 1861, and 6 lodging houses compared to 7 in 1861. Just 21% of the occupants were born in South Devon.

There were some interesting characters. William B Mallard, who lived in Number 2, was a Fellow of the College of Surgeons, and his neighbour in Number 3, was a retired army surgeon. Living in Number 6 was George Lang a Church of England Clergyman but no clue as to which church he was attached to.

In Number 8, lived Jagnetta Ellicombe aged 73 who was born in St Sidwell's, Exeter. She and her two servants had the whole house to themselves. Back in 1861 she was living in Number 10 Abbey Crescent with her mother Lucy Ellicombe, when Jagnetta was noted as 'deaf'. However, there is no record of her living in Abbey Crescent for example in 1891. Returning to Abbey Crescent she would not have noticed many changes to the seafront area, except maybe the fresh, clean air rather than one smelling of effluent.

Next to Number 1 Abbey Crescent is the Old Toll House (Figure 8), sometimes referred to as Dyer's Cottage. In the 1901 census the building was called Rock Cottage and John Dyer the town gardener, his wife and three children were living there. He was born in High Bickington in North Devon.

For 50 years Abbey Crescent had been a symbol of the growth of Torquay but also one of permanence because during its life thus far there had been little change to the seafront. But a new century would bring many changes to Abbey Crescent and one was the sound of the trams trundling past its doors. There had been plans to construct a tram line from the harbour to Torquay Station as early as 1859 and another attempt in 1876 that was thwarted by objectors who said that a tram line would interfere with the horses and carriages that trotted along the coast road.

It was not until 1901 that a tramway for Torquay was taken seriously. Members of the Council visited two towns and one city to inspect their systems: Wolverhampton, Rotherham and even Paris. It was decided that the Dolter surface contact system would be used, thus doing away with the need for ugly overhead lines.

On the 7 March 1907 the first three Torquay trams were introduced and in 1908 the line along the seafront was commissioned. Abbey Crescent now had the noisy trams trundling close to its front doors and windows. The vibrations from the trams and the squealing wheels on the curve of the bend would have annoyingly passed through the tarmac, pavements and air to the buildings. However, the safety of the surface contact system of powering the trams was poor. At least one horse was electrocuted.

Just two years later in 1910 it was decided that the trams should be powered via overhead lines and the installation of the street furniture commenced. Abbey Crescent now had the unsightly poles and wires just outside its front room windows as well as noisy trams trundling by. Peaceful Abbey Crescent had gone forever and would never return.

However, the trams had revolutionised travel in the town. An Abbey Crescent resident could now travel quickly to St Marychurch and the delights of Babbacombe or to Paignton. The last Torquay tram ran on 31 January 1934 and was replaced by the growing bus service.

Figure 9 – the new trams circa 1908 trundle past Abbey Crescent

In 1911 the building of the bathing platform along Abbey Sands commenced with its wide walkway and steps down to the beach or, at high tide to the sea. It took until the 1920s before it stretched along the full length of Abbey Sands, and is still an asset to the seafront area.

By 1920 the rear of Abbey Crescent had been in-filled with building extensions, although the front appeared unaltered. But by 1925 (Figure 10) there had been a roof extension providing a second floor rather than just loft rooms. Numbers 3 to 8 Abbey Crescent had become the Palm Court Hotel. The age of the Torquay tourist had arrived and the town had to provide for a mass market who came for a week or fortnight rather than cater just for the good and the great, and the rich and famous that came to Torquay to live or to overwinter.

Figure 10 also shows dozens of beach-goers enjoying Torre Abbey Sands as the tide rolled in. The Colonnade was built on the bathing platform in 1924. On its roof was a sun terrace and underneath was a takeaway café selling pots of tea, refreshments and ice creams. In the 1950s I watched in amazement how the café staff dried the plates and saucers at an astonishing rate, and how I longed to be bought an ice cream on a hot summer's day.

So the residents at Abbey Crescent and the guests at the Palm Court Hotel could benefit from the trams, Rock Walk, Old Maid's Perch, the slipway, the bathing platform, the Colonnade and be part of the hustle and bustle of crowds of holiday makers on the beach just across the road.

The growing tourist industry started to produce Torquay guides to publicise the town's facilities. The 1928/1929 guide (Figure 12) is an example and the Palm Court Hotel advertisement proudly states: 'superb position immediately in front of Torre Abbey Sands. The most convenient situation for every attraction or amusement that Torquay offers.'

The guide picture suggests that the ground floor has large bay windows and there is a roof extension in what were Numbers 6, 7 and 8 Abbey Crescent. We are also told that the hotel's facilities include: 'hot and cold running water, gas and electric fires in all bedrooms, individual attention, perfect cuisine, best English meat only and eggs from own farm'.

Figure 10 – In circa 1925 the trams are powered via overhead cables

Figure 11 – Old Maids Perch in the 1920s

By 1934 the trams have been replaced by the car and bus, and a terrace has been built in front of the hotel (Figure 14). The bathing platform extends all the way to Corbyn Beach. Figure 15 is seemingly, a perfect view of the promenade from Abbey Crescent and the Palm Court Hotel. It is mid-tide and the sands have no seaweed, Rock Walk is bathed in colour, the sun is shining and there are no traffic holdups. Even the Old Toll House has been painted. However, this is a coloured postcard and the road and beach are strangely the same incorrect colour. The beach sand is actually the colour of red sandstone.

**Figures 12 & 13 – The 1928/1929 Torquay Guide
(Alan Henshaw collection)**

Figure 14 – By circa 1934 the trams have gone and are replaced with the motor car

The road opposite the Old Toll House towards the harbour is now much wider (Figure 15) because between 1933 and 1934 significant land reclamation permitted the road and pavements to be widened and the sunken gardens to be built that run along the promenade to the Princess Theatre. This immediately became a very attractive asset to the seafront area. An additional benefit was the added protection for the road against the storms.

Figure 15 – another circa 1935 picture. The yellow building has been erected between the Crescent and the Old Toll House

Figure 16 - The helium balloon circa 2010   Figure 17 - The Abbey Gardens green 2020

In 1920 Torquay Borough Council bought a large square of Abbey Meadows bordering the seafront and Belgrave Road from the Cary family for £4,000 with the intention of making a public park. By 1922 the tennis courts, changing rooms and a tea house had been built. Then a miniature golf course was built on the section fronting the seafront (Figure 10) and beautiful ornamental gardens created behind and to the side. A bowling green was also constructed. The park's original name was Belgrave Gardens but now has the grander name of Abbey Park. By the 1930s the gardens facing the seafront were a beautiful park to relax in. It is still a very pleasant spot to visit.

The miniature golf course in time became a putting green and then, in 2008, this was swept away and the town's helium gas balloon was erected offering 15 minute 'flights' for £14. It was secured to the ground and merely flew 400 feet in a vertical direction by its pilot. However it was badly damaged in the storm of January 2012 and never flew again. The plot of land is now an uninteresting open public space with picnic tables (Figure 17).

Another pre-war scene (Figure 19) shows a busy Torre Abbey Sands. It's a great photo to note the original façade of the four end houses of Abbey Crescent, and the in-fill building between it and the Old Toll House. The crowds are packed against the Colonnade either expecting an imminent high tide or waiting for an outgoing tide. The disadvantage of Torre Abbey Sands as a tourist beach is that at high tide the sea laps at the bathing platform and for an hour or two the beach disappears under the waves.

Figure 18 – Abbey Gardens in 1936

Figure 19 – a busy pre-war Torre Abbey Sands

The 1939 Torquay Tourist guide (Figures 20 and 21) shows the further development of Abbey Crescent. There is a beer garden, a large awning and a raised rustic shelter next to Old Maid's Perch.

The ballroom looks palatial with latticed windows and a large ceiling skylight and diners had a wonderful view of the bay. The photo of the hotel exterior cleverly shows the road empty of cars. The brochure has a distinctly up-market feel about it and the hotel is telling the world that it has come of age. This is how it describes the hotel:

'So close to the seashore, almost level with its golden beach, yet commanding the whole sweep of Torbay. The cuisine expresses Devon hospitality. There is a Riviera sparkle in its atmosphere.'

Figures 20 & 21 – 1939 Torquay Guide advertisement (Alan Henshaw collection)

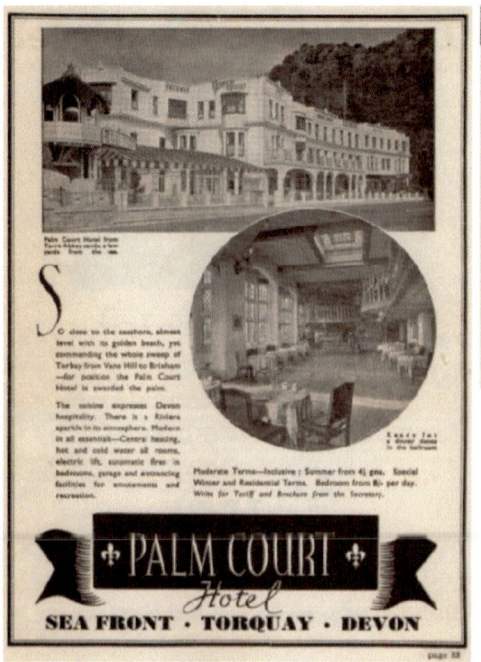

Figure 22– 1939 Palm Court Hotel advertisement (Source - Grace's Guide to British Industrial History)

Figure 23 is a pre-1934 view of a busy beach, the Colonnade and bathing tents lining the bathing platform. Along the coast road the tram line posts still stand and the road is empty. The small triangular garden at Old Maid's Perch that is squeezed between Sheddon Hill and Torbay Road is also visible.

During World War II many of our local hotels were requisitioned for use by the government. The Initial Training Wing for the RAF was stationed at Torquay and needed accommodation before being posted off for flight training. Torre Abbey Sands opposite the Palm Court Hotel was cordoned off by a high barbed wire fence for much of the war. However, the defences were very flimsy and wouldn't have presented any real obstacle for a determined invader. Then, at the end of the war, members of the Canadian Air Force were billeted at the Palm Court Hotel prior to being repatriated to Canada.

Figure 23 – a pre-1934 view of Torre Abbey Sands

Figure 24 – another pre-war scene

The postcard in Figure 24 is date stamped 1942 but must be a pre-war photo. I can't imagine hundreds of holiday makers being on the beach at the height of the conflict. The photo has it all. The coast road built in 1840, the widened road, pavement and sunken gardens completed in 1934, Rock Walk, the right hand side of Abbey Crescent that still retains its 1858 façade and the 1920s or 1930s in–fill building between it and the Old Toll House.

It shows the Palm Court Hotel building extensions and alterations that commenced in the 1920s and alongside it the small triangular garden and Old Maid's Perch given to the town in 1866 by R S S Cary. Then there is the slipway and the 1924 Colonnade.

Figure 25 is the hotel's advertisement in 1950. In the aftermath of the war, there are no over-the-top descriptions. It is stressing its excellent food, happy atmosphere and comfortable rooms. It is still a large hotel with 120 bedrooms.

Occasionally Torre Abbey Sands becomes covered in green seaweed brought in by the incoming tide. One commentator on seeing a green beach in a photograph said: 'this is a coloured photo rather than the original colour – the beach is not green'. The writer was of course incorrect. The seaweed is washed ashore by strong easterly winds and is deposited across the concrete steps waiting for an incoming tide to wash it out to sea or it is taken away by Council staff. I swam many times at high tide through such seaweed to get to the clear waters some thirty yards out to sea. The Colonnade itself was not the most hygienic of places and a childhood memory of it is the combined smell of sand, seaweed, stewed tea and dried urine. Despite this, days out at Torre Abbey Sands were very happy times.

Another unusual feature of Torre Abbey Sands are the small deposits of black sand. My father, a Torquay boatman, told me it was oil that had been washed up onto the beach from the engines of boats and ships. There is however, a more spectacular reason. Beneath the sands are the remains of a marshy woodland that grew 5,000 to 10,000 years ago. The black sand is decomposing wood from this forest. There are similar submerged forest beds at Goodrington.

Figure 25 – 1950 Palm Court Hotel advertisement
(Source - Grace's Guide to British Industrial History)

PALM COURT HOTEL
SEA FRONT — TORQUAY

Right by the Sands — No hills to Climb

Ideal for Summer and Winter Holidays

Over 120 Bedrooms all modern facilities. Lift. Central Heating. H. & C. in all Bedrooms. Cocktail Lounge. Billiard Room. Ballroom. Restaurant & Café.

Excellent Food, Courteous Service, Comfortable Rooms, and a happy atmosphere all its own, make the Palm Court THE most popular Hotel in Torquay.

Write for Illustrated Brochure & Tariff
Fully LICENSED   Phone : Torquay 4881 - 2

The Palm Court Hotel flourished in the 1950s and 1960s. Although I grew up in Torquay in those decades my interest in the hotel as a child and teenager was minimal. It was just a hotel that I walked past on my way to and from Torre Abbey Sands. Often I walked down Sheddon Hill to the beach, when not even the back of the hotel would have been noticed.

In the 1960s the hotel's front was nicely presented where guests could sit on the small pleasant terrace that ran parallel with the pavement and was potted out with large succulents and shrubs. Guests could look along the seafront road and admire the sunken gardens with their neatly mowed lawns, plenty of colourful flowers and the now famous palm trees (Figure 26). The gardens were part of the Torbay Road Improvement Scheme that was opened by the Minister of Transport on 8 June 1934 and a commemoration plaque is set into the sea wall near to the Torre Abbey Sands slipway (Figure 27).

Figure 26 – The sunken gardens

Around 1964 the hotel lift broke down during a wedding reception and the bride and groom were trapped for a while. They honeymooned in Africa where the groom was attacked and eaten by a lion and his body was never found. Also in 1964 the film 'The System', directed by Michael Winner, had a shot taken outside the entrance to the Palm Court Hotel where it appeared palatial compared to the photo taken many years later where the hotel looks tired and worn and might already be closed as a hotel (Figure 28).

Figure 29 suggests a thriving 1970s hotel. The 1939 beer garden in Figure 20 is now an indoor bar/café and on its flat-roofed terrace there is an outdoor bar/café. Both on this sunny summer's day are very busy and the hotel walls have been kept in a good state of repair. The roof extensions forming a second floor now extend right up to Number 5 Abbey Crescent. Numbers 3 and 4 would in time also have roof extensions.

Figure 27 – The 1934 Torbay Road Improvement plaque
Figure 28 – Palm Court Hotel entrance 2008 (Kind permission from reelstreets.com)

Figure 29 – Palm Court Hotel in the 1970s (Photo by Bendles Printers)

A welcome addition to the seafront scene was the construction in 1971 of the footbridge over the Torbay Road from the popular Old Maid's Perch to the beach. Its design won an award.

During the 1980s the Palm Court continued as a hotel. My son said this: 'I remember my Uncle Bruce staying there then when I was about eight years old. He said he was in the Palm Court and I was really worried because the only court I knew about was the type that sent you to prison.' A decade later the hotel had either been sold or had a change of use from a hotel to Mojo Café Bar. Life for Abbey Crescent would be different again. However, Numbers 1 & 2 Abbey Crescent remained in private ownership as separate cafés.

A memory from a Torquinian about the Mojo Cafe Bar in 1994 is this: 'Mojos was very popular especially in the summer where it got very cramped and sweaty and had loud music. It was very trendy and rowdy. I went there sporadically from about aged 16 until it shut I guess. The Mojo

Café Bar had regular bands and DJs and on hot summer days it would be full to capacity with people sitting on the terrace outside with their drinks.'

There was also during the 1990s the Captain Peppers bar that sold very cheap soft drinks for children and a play area which meant the adults could enjoy their drinks in relative peace and quiet. Across the road, the Colonnade, which had been neglected and was semi-derelict, was demolished in 1995. 71 years of the smell of sand, seaweed and dried urine were gone forever.

Figure 30 - Old Maid's Perch and the 1971 footbridge
(Photo by Colour Master International)

During the football World Cup in 2010 the Mojo Café Bar screened live football including the match between England v Algeria where the score was 0 – 0 and another game to be forgotten.

Then, two months later at 11.30 pm on 29 August 2010, there was a serious disorder at the Mojo Café Bar. The Torbay Council Licence Review, dated 2 September 2010, stated the incident involved a significant amount of patrons during which a female sustained serious facial injuries as result of a glass being thrown. There had been ongoing problems of overcrowding and stewarding issues including at the Young Farmers' spring event.

The Mojo Café Bar was forced to cease trading and it was the end of another chapter in the history of Abbey Crescent. Four months later at about 6.30 am on 18 December 2010 a devastating fire destroyed much of the old Palm Court Hotel. Six appliances from around the county tackled the blaze and mercifully the Devon and Somerset Fire and Rescue Service said it did not believe anyone had been in the building at the time of the fire. Onlookers described thick smoke and several loud bangs as the flames took hold. However, the fire did not spread to the far end of the crescent and thankfully Numbers 1 and 2 Abbey Crescent with much of their original façade were spared from the fire.

Two years later on 28 May 2012 the press reported that the hotel would be redeveloped following the sale of the site to Palm Court (Torquay) Ltd. The new development would also be known as Abbey Crescent and would include 14 holiday apartments, 14 residential apartments and 4 restaurants.

To the displeasure of many, three months earlier in February 2012 Torbay Council authorised the sale of 83 square metres of Old Maid's Perch to the new owners of the Palm Court Hotel. It was part of the land that was a gift to the town in 1866 as a public space and enjoyed by generations of residents and visitors.

Figure 31 – Old Maid's Perch in 2020

Six benches that had the best views of the beach (Figure 30) have now been lost and most of Old Maid's Perch is no more. It is now used as a restaurant terrace behind which are public seats but where the sea view is blocked (Figure 31). Ironically, a plaque celebrating the refurbishment of Old Maid's Perch in the centenary year of Torquay as a Borough in 1992 still remains.

However, the Abbey Crescent that had been built in 1858 and destroyed by fire would literally rise from the ashes to become Abbey Crescent once more. By 2015, the reincarnation of Abbey Crescent from an 1858 Regency-style building to a 21st-century Abbey Crescent was complete. Although the new building dwarfs the old Numbers 1 and 2 Abbey Crescent, it is a coming together of two different ages. In 1861 Number 1 Abbey Crescent was a lodging house and Number 2 was the home of a retired army lieutenant. 150 years later the new development is also mix of holiday apartments and homes. So in that sense nothing has changed.

Figure 32 – The old Numbers 1 & 2 Abbey Crescent in 2020

Figure 33 – 21C Abbey Crescent and the 20C bridge (photo by John Watt)

In 2021 the Old Toll House is undergoing change too. After a life of being a toll house, a home, a beach manager's office and public toilets it is currently standing empty and awaiting a new purpose and use for this mid-19th century building.

There is more to learn about Abbey Crescent. Further study is needed on Numbers 1 and 2 Abbey Crescent which are currently the On the Rocks restaurant and a fish and chip café to ascertain what remains of the 1858 building, and about the part it played in the two World Wars. That is for version two of this history.

Whatever we think of the old and the new buildings, the history of Abbey Crescent mirrors the history of Torquay. It follows the growth of the town, its transformation into a holiday destination and its desire to move with the times to serve the different generations over more than 160 years.

CHAPTER 3

A VISIT TO MEADFOOT AND DADDYHOLE PLAIN

Less than one mile east of Torquay Harbour are the attractive areas of Meadfoot and Daddyhole Plain. There is plenty to see and do on a short visit to this part of Torquay. It has high rugged cliffs, green wooded slopes, historic buildings, a sandy beach, stunning sea views and much more. It has over the years, despite urban development, retained its undoubted beauty.

During our visit we will follow in the footsteps of Sir James and Lady Morrison, a wealthy London couple who had a retirement holiday in Torquay in May and June 1851 and stayed at Hesketh Crescent that is in the Meadfoot area of the town.

The starting point for our tour is outside the centre house of Hesketh Crescent. After which we will walk around its grounds and visit the immediate area: Meadfoot Beach, Daddyhole Plain, the remnant of the Rock End Mansion Estate and hear the legend of the Demon Hunter of Devil's Hole and, if open, visit the National Coastwatch Institute Visitor Centre and finally, admire the 145-year-old coastguard station and cottages.

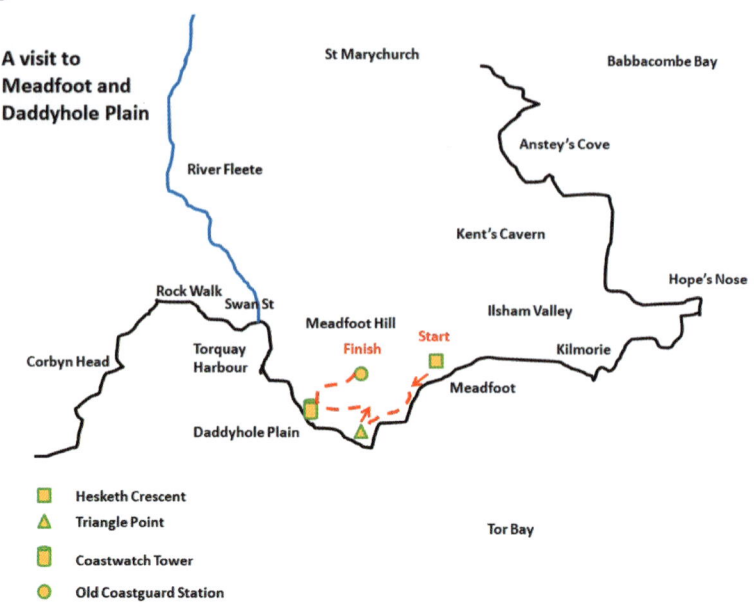

One of many remarkable aspects of Sir James's holiday is that he kept a journal which is held in the library of the Torquay Museum Society. It records where they stayed, where they went and what they did. He was born around 1774 and lived at a grand house called The Hermitage in the London suburb of Snaresbrook about 8 miles northeast of the centre of London. He had been Deputy Master of the Mint in Tower Hill and retired in 1850 aged 76. Then, having heard so much about Torquay from his Torquay friend and artist Frederick Stockdale, Sir James decided that 1851 was the right time for his retirement holiday. He writes:

'The coast of Devon has long been regarded for the mildness of its climate and for its beautiful scenery and long have my dear wife and I felt a wish to visit this lovely locality.'

After travelling to Torquay by train on 22 May 1851, the couple, along with six servants, first stayed at rented apartments in Livermead House which is now the Livermead House Hotel. However, Sir James was not all together happy with Livermead House. It was not he says: 'suitable for their needs' and I think he must have heard about Hesketh Crescent. He set off the following morning for Torquay town centre and on to Hesketh Crescent which overlooks its terraces and beautifully landscaped gardens that stretch down almost to Meadfoot Beach:

'We hired a carriage after breakfast for the purpose of seeing the town, and looking at the various villas, and whether we could procure a more eligible residence in Torquay.'

It is not surprising that Sir James was immediately impressed with Hesketh Crescent, an amazing Regency-style building now with Grade II* listed status. It overlooks Meadfoot Beach and has glorious sea views. He and Lady Morrison rented Number 1 for the remaining 12 days of their holiday. He describes Hesketh Crescent as 'magnificent'. It was and it still is:

'Magnificent Crescent adapted to the higher class of company. Mr Kirvey, the proprietor showed us three of the houses. Number 1 and 15 are superior, the last is superb. Number 15 was partly engaged, but Mr Kirvey the proprietor offered us Number 1, at 5 guineas a week.'

Outside of Number 8, which is the centre house and the grandest of all the 15 houses, is the Torbay Civic Society plaque recording that Hesketh Crescent was built by J T and W Harvey brothers in 1848. The crescent was commissioned by Sir Lawrence V Palk who lived in Number 15 and named after his grandson Lawrence Hesketh Palk who was born in 1846. Then on his death in 1860, his son Lawrence lived in Number 8 for a few years.

The second blue plaque commemorates the visit of Charles Darwin in 1861 when he stayed in Number 2 Hesketh Crescent. Imagine seeing this magnificent crescent in 1851 the year of Sir James's visit when it was almost new. At the time it was said that: 'the proportions are perfect and the quality of the ornamental stone and ironwork places the building in a class of its own'. Another commentator remarked that it was: 'the finest crescent of houses in the West of England'.

One only has to admire the building from either Meadfoot Sea Road, Meadfoot Beach or from right outside its front doors to agree with these seemingly over-the-top exaggerations. It is well-worth wandering along the outside to grasp its sheer scale and beauty.

Figure 35 – Hesketh Crescent 2020

Figures 36 and 37 – the blue plaques at Hesketh Crescent

In 1853, Number 8 Hesketh Crescent became the Osborne Hotel and it is still called that today making it one of the oldest hotels in Torquay. The first advertisement for the hotel was in the Torquay Directory newspaper for Wednesday 18 January 1854 and sums up the attraction of staying there.

> OSBORNE HOUSE,
> HESKETH CRESCENT.
> MRS. COTHER respectfully announces to the Nobility and Families of distinction visiting Torquay that she has Suites of Apartments vacant, replete with every comfort and convenience, (with private Board.) The Pleasure Grounds are beautifully laid out in Walks and Terraces, bordering the Ocean at the foot of Torbay, and are exclusively for the use of Visitors residing in the Crescent.

Figure 38 – Torquay Directory Newspaper 18 January 1854
(Torquay Museum Society Library)

Figure 39 - Hesketh Crescent 1848 (Torquay Museum Archive PR 35654)

The 1848 Victorian Magic Lantern slide of Hesketh Crescent (Figure 39) shows that the surrounding area is certainly unlike today. Then it was a treeless coastline and not one other house is in the vicinity and this suggests that it is one of the earliest pictures of Hesketh Crescent. A later 1867 picture has several houses above it and in the distance Kilmorie House. The cliffs are now wooded and the hills are dotted with houses and apartment blocks. Sir James writes in his diary about the view from the garden:

'From the grounds there is a beautiful prospect of the bay with three island rocks which form interesting objects.'

He was referring to Orestone, Thatcher Rock and Shag Rock. Figure 40 shows Orestone in the distance, the triangular Thatcher Rock and the smaller Shag Rock in the foreground. My father was a Torquay boatman and he told me that to avoid the rocks between Thatcher Rock and Thatcher Point, he had to steer a route a distance from Thatcher Rock 'that you can throw a biscuit'. He was of course referring to the biscuit or tack, eaten for centuries by sailors. In the 21st-century skippers sail their pleasure boats on the seaward side of Thatcher Rock avoiding the requirement to hone their biscuit throwing skills.

Figure 40 – The three islands rocks and Triangle Point from Daddyhole Plain

We will now wander along the pavement to the far end of Hesketh Crescent and stand outside Number 15. During his holiday Sir James was desperate to look inside Number 15 and I do wonder if he dreamt of it being his retirement home but as far as I know he never returned to Torquay, and his retirement was lived out at Snaresbrook rather than Hesketh Crescent.

Number 15 is, after the central house, the grandest of the other 14 houses. It is quieter with no horses clip-clopping past, it's nearer to the sea and enjoys the sunset. It has impressive external features: wonderful cornices, a double front door and a carving of a friendly local above it.

Before we walk down to Meadfoot Beach we will retrace our steps and stop outside Number 1 Hesketh Crescent where Sir James and Lady Morrison stayed. In Sir James's words it was superior and indeed it was and still is, having much of the architectural detail found in Number 15.

Hesketh Crescent remains one of Torquay's iconic buildings. In 2021 the Osborne Hotel still has its main entrance at Number 8, the grandest of all the houses and has 33 bedrooms that stretch over 4 of the original houses. 8 of the 15 houses are now occupied by the self-catering resort of 46 apartments, and the remaining 3 houses have been converted into private apartments.

Figure 41 – Architechtural details of Number 15 Hesketh Crescent

Figure 42 – Number 1 Hesketh Crescent

We will now walk down through the gardens of Hesketh Crescent and through the thoughtfully positioned pedestrian entrance to Meadfoot Sea Road and stand on the Meadfoot Beach slipway. Two years after

Hesketh Crescent was completed the first sea road was built in 1850 but was washed away that same year. The rebuilt road was also washed away, this time, in the Great Storm of 1859. By 1867 Kilmorie House at the far end of the beach had been built and replaced in the 1960s by the huge block of white apartments which can be seen in Figure 40.

The present road with its substantial sea wall was completed in 1878 and in it is a huge pipe that took the Torquay sewage via a tunnel to Hope's Nose. Prior to this, Torquay's sewage entered the sea at three places: near Corbyn Head, near the seafront junction with Belgrave Road and an outlet near to the Pavilion causing Torre Abbey Sands and the harbour area to be highly polluted.

A major engineering scheme piped the sewage away from the seafront and harbour area to Hope's Nose. The old sewage outlets on the seafront were connected to a new pipe at the base of Rock Walk and piped via a tunnel through Rock Walk to a pumping station at Swan Street, then via a long tunnel through Meadfoot Hill to Meadfoot Sea Road. A third tunnel was built from Kilmorie to Hope's Nose. Prior to its opening in August 1878, guests walked through this last tunnel with the entire length laid with boards and candles. The new sewage system meant no more noxious smells on Torquay seafront. The 1878 sewage scheme was in use until 2002 when the modern sewage treatment plant at Churston was opened and since then all the Torquay sewage is now piped away from the town. No more extremely unpleasant smells at Hope's Nose and a clean sea and clean beaches.

The slipway at Meadfoot was built either in 1878 or in 1884 when the road was strengthened. For many years the beach had bathing machines secured by long ropes tied to wooden stakes fixed to the cliffs and were manhandled as the tide changed so that they were always at the water's edge. Originally they were for the exclusive use of the Osborne Hotel guests. Over the years the beach promenade and beach cafe have steadily improved. For example, in the early 1930s there were beach huts along the new promenade.

The most recent development at Meadfoot Beach, other than ongoing repairs to the sea defences, was in 2015 when the 69 beach huts were replaced by 137 modern chalets over two storeys. Despite the estimated cost by Torbay Council of at least £250,000, the final bill was £2,000,000 and this works out to £14,500 per chalet. The council was criticised by the press for spending four times more on beach huts than it did on affordable housing in three years.

Figure 43 – Meadfoot Beach circa 1901

Figure 44 – Meadfoot Beach in the 1930s

Figure 45 – Meadfoot Beach 2020 and the headland called Triangle Point

One 19th-century feature usually missed on Meadfoot Sea Road is the old drinking fountain. It is set into the cliff below Hesketh Crescent and fed by the Meadfoot Spring that flows at the surface just behind it. Unfortunately the water from the spring is now polluted and we are informed by Torbay Council via a notice fixed to the fountain that: 'The purity of this water cannot be Guaranteed'. The last word really does have a capital G.

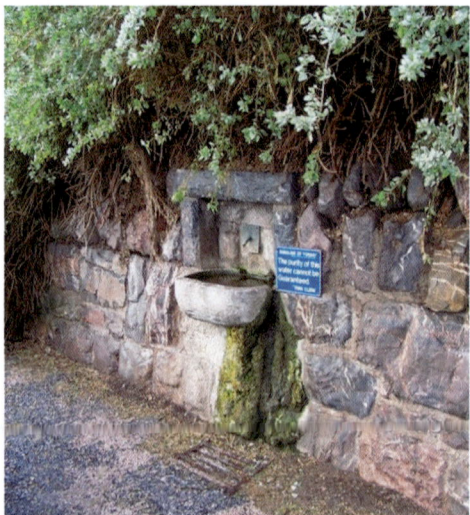

Figure 46 – Meadfoot Sea Road Drinking Fountain

There was also a second and little-known drinking fountain that right up to the 1970s Torquinians would fill up bottles of its water to drink on the beach or to take home. An Exeter doctor even collected water from it and he advised his patients to do likewise because of its medicinal qualities. Now long gone and almost forgotten the drinking fountain was set into the Hesketh Crescent garden wall a few yards down from the pedestrian gate where its bricked up arch can be seen (Figure 47). At the top of the wall is a pipe from which the water trickles into a 50 cm by 50 cm shaft and the water was collected from pavement level. The shaft is surprisingly 10 metres deep (Figure 48) and enters the large tunnel at Meadfoot Beach to drain into the sea.

On their first Sunday morning Sir James and Lady Morrison attended a service at St John's Church, then after lunch walked along Meadfoot Beach. That day he describes Daddyhole Plain in his diary:

'On the west side of the crescent rises a precipitous hill, at the summit of which is the lofty Down of Daddy's Hole... In the evening we partly ascended the height of Daddy's Hole.'

Figure 47 and 48– The bricked up arch of the second drinking fountain and its 10 metre shaft

Walking up towards Daddyhole Plain, Sir James and Lady Morrison would have looked back towards Number 1 Hesketh Crescent, and admired their holiday home. He uses the name Daddy's Hole which is the old name for Daddyhole Plain, and the even older name is Devil's Hole, and it is the place of the 'Legend of Torquay and The Demon Hunter'. It's unlikely that Sir James had heard this story because it only came to light in 1850 in a book entitled 'Legends of Torquay'.

Figure 49 – Partial ascent to Daddyhole Plain circa 1910

The footpath up to Daddyhole Plain shown in Figure 49 still exists, although in 2021 the views of Hesketh Crescent and the sea are restricted because of the growth of trees. Sir James had a tremendous view not only of Hesketh Crescent including Number 15 on the far right of the crescent that he had set his heart on, but also Meadfoot Beach and those three island rocks of Orestone, Thatcher Rock and Shag Rock.

Part way up the path to Daddyhole Plain is a side path to a view point from where, looking far down to the sea, one can see the western end of Meadfoot Beach and Triangle Point (Figures 40 and 45). Triangle Point is a tricky place to get to from the beach because of the rocks sloping sides and it is dangerously difficult from the view point where it would be a precarious scramble. Triangle Point and the adjoining Knolls Quarry are important sites within the English Riviera UNESCO Global Geopark. For example, on the surface of the sloping limestone rocks of Triangle Point there are fossil corals from the 400 million year old Devonian reefs.

Figure 50 –Knoll Quarry

Knoll Quarry, located higher up the cliff from Triangle Point, is a worked out quarry where in 1889 a small amount of gold was found in the 'contorted and brecciated zone'. But beware - if you venture over there and extract any gold you will be fined anything from £20,000 to a fine with no upper limit. It's amazing that in the 19th century the quarrying industry was active all around the coastline of Torquay. Looking across from Knoll

Quarry towards the cliffs of Daddyhole Plain there is a real sense of the ruggedness, the height and danger of the cliffs.

From the view point we now walk further up the steep hill from Meadfoot and reach Daddyhole Plain where we are greeted by the views in an easterly direction shown in Figure 40 and the southern views shown in Figure 51, where the Coastwatch Station and its volunteers are safeguarding Tor Bay.

Daddyhole Plain is an expanse of flat grassland several acres in size with a dozen or so parking places. It's a superb place to sit and look out to sea or to start a coast path walk towards Torquay Harbour in one direction, or to Meadfoot Beach and beyond in the other direction.

A print of circa 1867 (Figure 52) shows a very different Daddyhole Plain from the one we recognise in the 21st century. It wasn't a flat field of grass, but a terrain more like Wall's Hill in Babbacombe with tuffs of grass, gorse bushes and no doubt plenty of blackberry bushes. The print also shows Daddyhole Cove at its base and people walking on it. In December 1876 a young servant woman decided to clamber down to the cove from Daddyhole Plain. Unfortunately she took the wrong path, slipped and 'rolled from rock to rock until she reached the bottom, a depth of nearly two hundred feet'. Incredibly she survived the fall after being helped by a butler, some quarrymen and men on a small boat who rowed her around to Meadfoot Beach.

Figure 51 – Daddyhole Plain and the National Coastwatch Institute tower

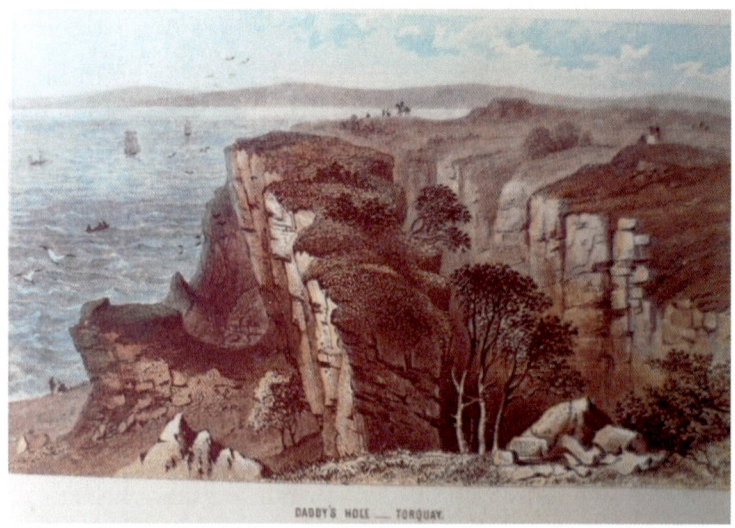

Figure 52 – Daddy's Hole circa 1867 (Torquay Museum Society Library)

Over the last 170 years rock falls have swept away the footpath to Daddyhole Cove and covered the cove with huge rocks making it now totally inaccessible. The massive tower of rock and chasm is less easy to pick out now, owing to rock falls and the increase in vegetation but it is visible from the cliff edge just beyond the right-hand side of the car park. Figure 52 also shows a rider on a horse by the cliff edge who is looking out to sea, and it is a scene like this that stirred the imagination and creativity of two 19th-century South Devon writers and poets.

The 1850 anonymous book the 'Legends of Torquay' has a story that is centred around Daddyhole Plain and the chasm of 'Devil's Hole'. And it is in that chasm down to the sea where the Devil is said to live. The heroine in the legend is called Matilda who is a young single woman and is looking for a husband.

In 1888 the story was embellished and turned into a poem by Thomas Aggett. He gets his inspiration not only from Daddyhole Plain and its old name of the Devil's Hole, but also from Ilsham Valley and its woods that stretch up either side of the road to Wellswood from the other end of Meadfoot Beach and, from a small castle-like structure called The Lookout on the coast path between Daddyhole Plain and Torquay Harbour. It is to The Lookout where we will now walk, by passing the Coastwatch Station and following the coast path for a few hundred yards whilst admiring the stunning views of Tor Bay.

Figure 53 – the view from the coast path Lookout across Tor Bay

Figure 54 – the Lookout

The Lookout is a remnant of the 20-acre Rock End Mansion Estate that stretched between Daddyhole Plain and the Imperial Hotel. It was the home of Lord Beverley and was built sometime before 1841. Sir James and Lady Morrison visited the 16-bedroomed Rock End Mansion and were extremely impressed with its gardens and location. He says that it was much superior to nearby Woodbine Cottage, 'particularly in respect to the fine prospect it commands'. It certainly was in a beautiful location and the coast path provides us with the identical views across Tor Bay 170 years later.

In 1905 the estate was up for sale and the sale brochure states that it was: 'remarkably beautiful and very valuable' and that it was 'within a few minutes' walk of the town'. Well not really, it is a good 15 to 20 minutes walk. The estate still existed in 1947 but by the early 1960s it had been sold for house building. The arrangement was that F T Stoneman Ltd, a prestigious Torquay house building firm, would build the homes in Rock End Avenue and the adjoining roads, with the cliff edge being transferred to Torquay Council after which the coast path was constructed for all to enjoy.

Thomas Aggett the creator of the 'Demon Hunter' poem was dubbed the 'Railway Poet' and, despite being an ordinary working man, in his case a porter at Teignmouth Railway Station he became an accomplished poet. He was born in Cornwall and grew up in Torquay with his mother and younger brother. The 1871 census reveals that he lived in 7 Madrepore Road, Torquay where there were 5 households and 14 people living in this one house. It is situated in the Pimlico area which at the time was a poor part of the town. In 1880, aged 17, Thomas moved to the Isle of Wight to become a footman to a wealthy woman. It was here that his love of literature grew and blossomed because his employer had a large library and Thomas was determined to use all his spare time reading.

He became a devotee of Burns and Byron who were his inspiration to be a poet. After two years work on the Isle of Wight, Thomas returned to Devon and took up his post of porter at Teignmouth Railway Station and remained in this job right up to his retirement. His hobby and pastime became poetry. He said that he wanted to show that Devon can produce something besides clotted cream.

And one of his two poetry books, 'The Demon Hunter - a legend of Daddy's Hole Plain, Torquay' was published in 1888 by the Widows' and Orphans' Fund of the Great Western Railway. Thomas Aggett has taken the legend of Matilda in the 1850 book and written a monumental poem of 113 verses, each with 8 lines and all written in a fortnight's holiday.

Thomas also uses his knowledge of the classics learnt from the books in the library of his employer on the Isle of Wight. He changes the heroine's name from Matilda to Proserpine, the Roman Goddess of the underworld. Proserpine is not married and she decided that a suitor would have to win her love by showing their bravery and horsemanship by riding around the battlements of her father's castle. Imagine, as you read the early verses of Thomas Aggett's poem, a knight riding a horse around the battlements of the Daddyhole Lookout:

> 'Her father's castle stood on a mound,
> And anyone upon its outer wall
> Would shudder and remark on looking round,
> If any Knight should from it chance to fall,
> He'd get an irrecoverable wound
> And would not stand the slightest chance at all,
> Having fallen down from where he lay to rise
> Much less to claim fair Proserpine as his prize.'

Many knights attempted the challenge and failed and fell to their death until a knight from King Arthur's Round Table arrived:

> 'A moment later on the castle wall
> She saw in seeming confidence appear,
> The noble steer with careful tread, now all
> Is dazed before her by each binding tear.
>
> She dried her eyes and now again observed
> The battlements, and still the Knight was there,
> The steer and rider seemed iron nerved
> Proceeding steadily with such great care.'

The knight from King Arthur's Round Table had completed the challenge and having ridden around the castle walls he could claim Proserpine as his own. However, he tells her that he is already engaged to one who loves him and who did not set such a plan as hers that killed so many of his fellow knights. As the knight departs for his journey back to Cornwall, he leaves her with the words:

> 'So may the devil take thee for thy pains,
> For hell alone can purify thy stains.'

Proserpine is heartbroken and that evening she is alone on Daddyhole Plain brooding over the events of the day which is where we will return to hear the remainder of the story.

> 'Proserpine could not forget the Knight,
> Whose parting words had made her feeling smart,
> She would have vengeance, cost her what it might,
> If with her own life-blood she had to part.
> And she was still so deep in thought, when lo!
> She heard a blast as from a hunter's horn.'

Now imagine Proserpine watching a hideous figure riding his horse across Daddyhole Plain with his hounds running alongside him and rapidly approaching her:

> 'The Demon Hunter, mounted on a steed,
> Whose breath was fire, and when the Demon blew
> His horn, much fire did from that horn proceed.
> A couple of hounds with a flaming breath that flew.'

Terrified, Proserpine faints and after some time she comes round to find a handsome young stranger comforting her. He asks her what is the matter and she explains her challenge to her suitors of riding a horse around the castle battlements and how she was jilted by a knight of King Arthur's Round Table and her wish to take her revenge against him.

He listens intently and then makes a pact with her. He says that if he helps her take revenge she must marry him, despite her not knowing anything about him. Surprisingly Proserpine agrees and they arrange to meet up a few evenings later. When they rendezvous he tells her this:

> 'In yonder valley thou wilt find the Knight
> Thy former lover now in converse sweet
> With his fair lady, he enamoured quite
> Of her fair charms, is laying at her feet.
>
> The contract which we made the other night
> 'Tis scarcely necessary to repeat,
> Here is a dagger thou may'st now proceed,
> Naught now remains but to perform the deed.'

The 'yonder valley' that the handsome young stranger is referring to is the 600 yard long Ilsham Valley also known as Ilsham Green (Figure 55). It is enclosed on both sides by wooded hills and although the eastern side does have homes alongside the road, in my opinion this does not detract from its undoubted attractiveness.

Figure 55 – Ilsham Valley looking towards the sea

Proserpine is now completely under the spell of the stranger and still being full of revenge takes the dagger, goes to 'yonder valley' and hides in the bushes waiting for her moment:

> 'Forward she sprang, and in a moment she
> Had thrust the dagger through the heart of each.'

The evil deed has been done and Proserpine has had her revenge. She returns to Daddyhole Plain and searches for the handsome young stranger where, in the distance she thought she saw something or someone:

> 'She fainted not however now, nor ran,
> But stood transfixed with horror and surprise
> For she beheld the stranger, mortal man
> He was not, but the demon in disguise.
>
> Over the plain like hunted deer she flew,
> The Demon Hunter and his hounds pursued.
> Unequal was the chase, the distance grew
> Nearer and nearer, which the Demon viewed
> And forward pressed, a dreadful blast he blew
> From forth his horn, which often he renewed,
> The hellish sounds fair Proserpine alarms,
> And soon the Demon has her in his arms.
>
> The restless steed now struck the earth, and lo!
> A fearful chasm in the ground appeared
> In which he leapt, from the abyss below
> A thousand flames into the darkness reared
> And even then was heard, the Demon blow,
> A long last blast, as, midst the flames he steered,
>
> The Demon's voice was heard above the storm,
> 'Mine, mine.' he cried, 'Aye, aye, forever mine,
> Thou'lt reign in hell, a second Proserpine.'

Often, says the author of that 1850 book, 'The Legends of Torquay', that when the nights are dreary and dark, and the cold wind blows across the lonely Devil's Hole Plain, one should listen for the cries of the wretched young woman, as her destroyer pursues her tortured spirit over the dismal scene of that foul deed.

However, there is no need to wait for a dark and dreary night - go to Daddyhole Plain any day and peer over the railings on the right hand side of the car park, look down into the chasm of Devil's Hole and imagine Proserpine in its depths in the arms of the Demon Hunter.

One final thought about the poem 'The Demon Hunter, a Legend of Torquay'. It demonstrates the brilliance of Thomas Aggett the boy who grew up in a crowded house in a poor part of Torquay and became an accomplished poet. It is his legacy to perpetuate a story that will in the centuries to come be thought of as a legend from the mists of time.

There is still much more to be seen on this history visit to Daddyhole Plain. If it was the 1880s or later, we could drink from the fountain erected circa 1879. If it was the 1890s we could watch the St Mark's Church rugby team play other local teams and I dread to think who retrieved the ball when it was kicked over the cliff edge. And in the 1920s and 1930s we could have admired a World War I tank that stood on the Plain as a memorial, but was removed in World War II and presumably melted down. John Lipscombe my uncle now 99 years old remembers it well. In the 2010s we could visit the Coastwatch Visitor Centre, but unfortunately in 2020 it was closed due to the COVD-19 pandemic restrictions.

It's now time to wander from the chasm and the Coastwatch Visitor Centre towards the old coastguard cottages and coastguard station that are on the far side of Daddyhole Plain (Figure 57). They were built in 1875 and at the time it was cheaper to build the cottages than provide rented accommodation in the town for the coastguards to live in.

Between 1856 and 1923 the Coastguard Service was under the control of the Admiralty and the Daddyhole coastguard station was part of the Shore Force. Its duties included revenue protection i.e., detecting smuggling activities, and life saving in collaboration with the RNLI after Torquay's first lifeboat 'The Mary Brundret' was launched and stationed at Beacon Cove in May 1876.

By 1877 the Daddyhole Plain coastguard station was well and truly operational. The 'Torquay Times' and 'South Devon Advertiser' reported that on Thursday morning of the 24 May 1877 Rear-Admiral Augustus Phillimore, Admiral Superintendant of Naval Reserves visited Torquay and inspected and drilled the Torquay Division of the Coastguard Service who would have worn their naval-style uniforms. He also visited the station at Daddyhole Plain and the coastguards newly built boathouse on Haldon Pier.

The coastguard station and cottages were built before there was vehicular access to Daddyhole Plain and were approached by a footpath in Daddyhole Road that still has its blue, tiled sign. It looks like the back lane to the cottages, but is in fact a footpath leading to the front of the properties and their front doors. On the other side of the footpath are small gardens in which stand 10 semi-detached out-houses with chimneys which were the original 'wash-houses' – one for each cottage. Each windowless wash-house had a toilet (minus a hand basin), a small storeroom and a larger room where the clothes were laundered. The back of the original ten cottages look out across Daddyhole Plain and the doors on this side are all later additions.

Figure 56 – The Torquay Coastguards circa 1895 outside the boathouse
(Torquay Museum Archive PR25007a)

Figure 57 – the 10 coastguard cottages

The three-storey property was both the coastguard station and home of the Coastguard Chief Officer. The coastguard station was on the ground floor and an upper floor provided a viewing platform out across the bay.

The Coastguard Chief Officer and his family also lived on the upper floors. When the coastguards were needed in an emergency the Coastguard Chief Officer, or his deputy, could quickly run along the outside of the terrace and knock on the front doors to alert his team. The Coastguard Chief Officer is also said to have walked up the lane each day to check that the wives were working hard and being industrious. The ten coastguard cottages were all sold together as one lot for £6,000 between 1948 and 1949 and have since been reconfigured into eight private homes.

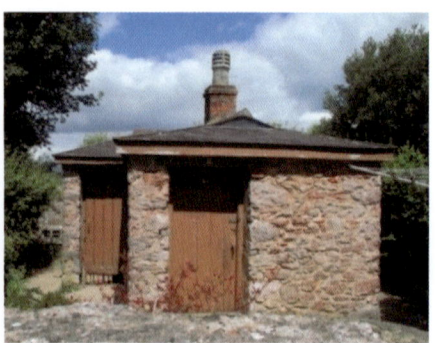

Figure 58 – the footpath to old Daddyhole Coastguard Station   Figure 59 – the wash-houses

It's not clear exactly when the first coastguard lookout station was built. An 1887 map of the Rock End Estate shows the cottages but no lookout tower. In the early days the coastguards would have sat on the top of the cliffs and watched the coast using telescopes. The OS maps published in 1906, 1935 and 1949 all show a coastguard lookout on the site of the Coastwatch tower and the cottages are labelled as the Coastguard Station.

A volunteer at the coastguard lookout in the late 1950s was Fred King. He was a summer crew member on the 'Pride of Paignton' pleasure boat and spent many happy hours out of season in the coastguard lookout safeguarding Tor Bay. Fred would have watched out for my father Raymond Badcott as he plied between Torquay Harbour and the beaches of Babbacombe as the skipper of the White Heather and Seacrest pleasure boats. Little did Fred know that he was watching over the future father-in-law of his son Colin King.

In the early 1960s the coastguard lookout was still manned, but a change of coastguard policy where the priorities changed from coastal watch in coastguard stations to one of remote monitoring of ships' movements from Maritime Rescue Coordination Centres resulted in the closure of the coastguard lookout tower. The tower at Daddyhole Plain was subsequently demolished as was the one at Hope's Nose. But like many aspects in life, things can turn full circle and with the closures of many coastguard stations serious concerns were being raised over sea safety and coastal protection. Then, following the loss of two Cornish fishermen in full view of a recently closed coastguard station, matters came to a head. From ensuing discussions the Coastwatch organisation was officially 'born' on Saturday 18 October 1994. Bass Point off the Lizard peninsular became the first working station and many others along the English and Welsh coastline have since been created.

Following a meeting chaired by Jon Gifford, the National Coastwatch Institute chairman at the Royal Torbay Yacht Club, proposals were put forward to open a station for the Torbay area. As mentioned the previous old watchtower had been demolished and a Torbay Coastwatch station was opened in 2009 on the footprint of the previous building. So began the recruitment and training of volunteers. The impressive Visitor Centre was built by the station manager Andy Milner and opened in 2014 by Commanding Officer, Captain Henry Duffy from The Britannia Royal Naval College in Dartmouth.

Our visit to Meadfoot and Daddyhole Plain is at an end, but we can continue to enjoy the area by retracing our steps to the Rock End Estate Lookout and walking another ½ mile along the coast path to Torquay Harbour or by walking back to Meadfoot Beach and Hesketh Crescent to enjoy once more the glorious views of Tor Bay from that vantage point.

For Sir James and Lady Morrison their holiday, which they had thoroughly enjoyed, would soon come to an end and the final paragraph in his holiday journal describes Torquay's early summer weather and the variety and beauty of the area. His last sentence certainly sums up how I feel about my visits to Meadfoot and Daddyhole and I do hope that you have enjoyed your visit too:

'We had been blessed with the most lovely weather during our sojourn at Torquay. No rain, the vegetation had been refreshed by the copious nightly dews, no rough or boisterous wind, but the gentle breeze of the sea. A temperature oppressive by neither heat nor cold but generally brilliant sun and occasional soft fleecy clouds. We are indeed thankful that we had thus been permitted to view this fair and beautiful scenery.'

<u>Dedication</u> - This study of Meadfoot and Daddyhole Plain is dedicated to Helen Cooper for the information provided about the Coastwatch station and to Joan Henshaw for her contribution about the Meadfoot drinking fountains.

CHAPTER 4

A DAY OUT IN THE 19TH CENTURY PARISH OF ST MARYCHURCH

'The sea, always the sea, nothing but the sea.' These were the words of Sir Edmund Gosse when recalling glimpsing the sea at Babbacombe Bay for the first time. He and his father Philip had moved from London to St Marychurch in 1857, when Edmund was 8 years old. Just imagine the feelings of a child who until that day had never ever seen the sea.

So what better way is there to find out what the parish of St Marychurch was like in the mid-19th century than through the eyes of those who lived in or visited this wonderful part of Torquay as Edmund Gosse? I don't think there is a better way. We are going to have a day out in the parish and find out what it was like by following in the footsteps of six 19th-century residents and visitors: Philip & Edmund Gosse, Matthew Bridges, Sir James and Lady Morrison and Prince Albert.

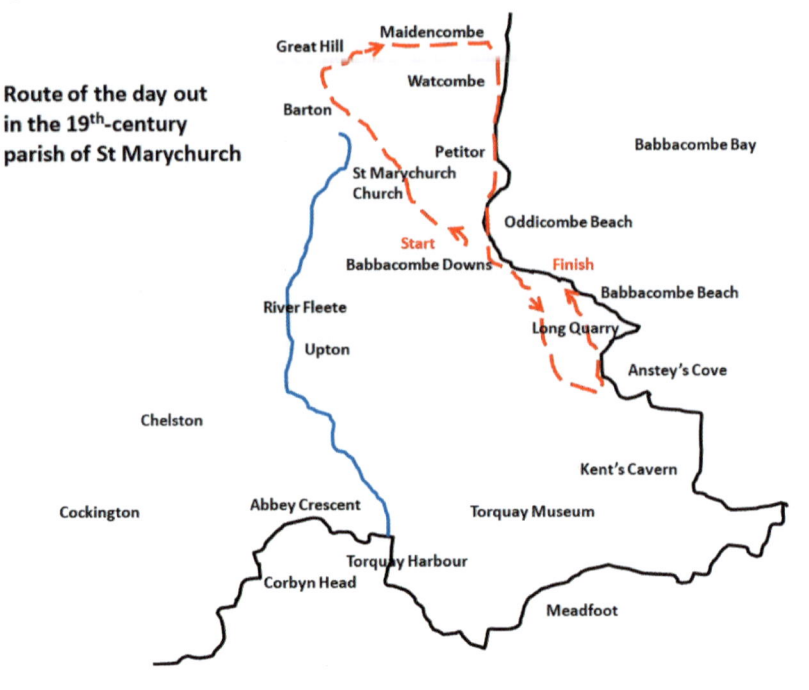

We will commence our tour on Babbacombe Downs and then walk through St Marychurch, Watcombe, Barton, Great Hill, Maidencombe, Watcombe Beach, Petitor Beach, Oddicombe Beach, Long Quarry, Anstey's

Cove and finish, probably exhausted, but hopefully exhilarated at Babbacombe Beach. Before we start out, here is a pen picture of those 19th-century inhabitants and visitors.

Father and son Philip and Edmund Gosse lived in St Marychurch from 1857. Later in life Edmund (who became Sir Edmund Gosse) wrote about his life as a child in St Marychurch and the biography of his marine zoologist father. Both books and those written by Philip Gosse have wonderful descriptions of the area which we will dip into.

Between 1840 and 1842, hymn writer Matthew Bridges visited Torquay and Babbacombe became his paradise. He wrote an atmospheric poem describing Babbacombe, Watcombe and Maidencombe inspired by his solitary walks in the vicinity of those beautiful spots.

Sir James and Lady Morrison were a wealthy London couple who had a two-week holiday in Torquay in 1851. They stayed at 1 Hesketh Crescent and tell us in their holiday diary about their visits to St Marychurch and Babbacombe with some interesting insights of the area.

Queen Victoria and Prince Albert were married in 1840, three years after she came to the throne. They visited Babbacombe twice. The first occasion was in 1846 and again in 1852. Prince Albert had tea at the Cary Arms at Babbacombe Beach and visited the marble works in St Marychurch.

On a personal note, seven generations of my family have lived near and loved the Babbacombe Downs and Beach. The first was my great-great grandfather Francis Eales who was born in 1826. He was a quarryman and lived for much of his life literally a stone's throw away from Babbacombe Downs. The last generation thus far is my grandson born in 2011.

In first half of the 19th century the parish of St Marychurch in Torquay was large and stretched from Ilsham and almost to Maidencombe, and included the areas of Barton and Shiphay too. Then, with the huge population growth of Torquay in the 19th century the parish was split into the new parishes of Babbacombe, Wellswood, St Marychurch, Barton and Shiphay. So what did 19th-century St Marychurch look like for these six residents and visitors? White's Devonshire Directory of 1850 describes it as:

'A handsome village and a picturesque parish, with many neat mansions and marine cottages. It includes the hamlets of Babbicombe, Barton, Combe Pafford, Edginswell and Collaton Shiphay, and is situated near the bold and rugged rocky cliffs of the southern recess of Babbicombe Bay.'

Now try to imagine for example, Matthew Bridges in 1842 aged 42, Sir James Morrison in 1851 aged 77, and Edmund Gosse in 1857 aged 8, all on Babbacombe Downs and peering over the cliffs to Babbacombe Beach. All were drawn to it, just as I am and no doubt you will be too on your day out. Figure 60 is the Babbicombe Beach that they would have seen. (I've used the old spelling for Babbacombe)

Figure 60 – Babbicombe Beach circa 1870 (Torquay Museum Society Library)

There is the wooded hollow leading down to a thatched Cary Arms. The Glen, previously called 'Babbacombe', with its Garden Room and boathouse perched right on the beach where Miss Emma Keyse was murdered in 1884 by John Lee. The house at the top of the hill was, to add confusion, also called The Glen and its owner Mr Tollemache was not happy that Miss Keyse had stolen the name. There is no Babbacombe Pier. This was not built until 1890 and its main use was 'to provide shelter for the fishermen's boats and gear'. However, at the official opening on Sunday 4 August 1890 there were no fishermen present. The officiating vicar expressed regret about this but added that if there had been fishermen there, including my great uncle Sam Badcott aged 18 and my great uncle John Badcott aged 23 years, he would have pointed out the evil of fishing on a Sunday.

White's 1850 Directory mentions that there were many neat mansions in St Marychurch. One was Sandhurst in St Marychurch Road, the home of Philip and Edmund Gosse. Philip bought it brand new and moved in when the plaster was still damp. Despite being a large house, they called it: 'our little house or villa'. It still exists and the main entrance is opposite Priory Road. Now extended and converted into apartments it is unrecognisable when compared to Figure 61. The Torbay Civic Society plaque commemorating Philip Gosse is at the Manor Road entrance. To understand what the Gosse's home was like, walk a few houses along where there is a Grade II listed and largely unaltered circa 1850 villa.

Figure 61 – 19C Sandhurst in St Marychurch

Figure 62 – Hampton House in circa 1917 (Image Terry Leaman)

The largest of all the mansions was Hampton House opposite the junction of St Marychurch Road and Fore Street but hidden by a high wall. Its 28-acre grounds included a farm, parkland that stretched to the cliffs above Oddicombe Beach and a long private driveway that commenced at what is now the junction of Babbacombe Road and Babbacombe Downs Road. Hampton House is now the Abbey School.

Hampton House was built circa 1820 and purchased in 1851 by Charles Tayleur who made a vast fortune building locomotives in his Vulcan Foundry in Warrington and exporting them around the world. The house remained in the Tayleur family until 1913 when the estate was sold to Mr Theo Foster a solicitor, who had plans to create a 'garden city'. The 'Torquay Directory' newspaper reported on 25 February 1914 that the estate: 'will provide building sites for scores of villas and bungalows'. The homes would be: 'designed artistically and provided with red-tiled roofs and it is also hoped that the scheme will include the erection of a fine hotel'.

World War I put an end to Mr Foster's plans and after the war was over he sold on his interest in the estate after which many of the existing houses were built in the 1920s with further additions at later dates. The buildings erected on the old estate include the shops and houses alongside Abbey School right up to Babbacombe Downs Road, Hampton Avenue, Cliffside Road, Higher Downs Road and the properties in Babbacombe Downs Road between Higher Downs Road and Babbacombe Road.

White's Directory also mentioned 'many marine cottages' and many still exist. For example, Homefield Terrace is tucked behind Babbacombe Downs Road and was built in the early to mid 19th century. The terrace in Cary Road (Figure 63) opposite the coastguard cottages was built between 1830 and 1860. It has been renamed Babbacombe Downs Road and it's where my great-great grandfather Francis Eales and my great grandfather George Badcott and their families lived two doors from each other in the 1860s. It really is a stone's throw from Babbacombe Downs.

Figure 63 – 19C Marine Cottages in Cary Road

On the 19 July 1852 Queen Victoria and Prince Albert visited Babbacombe on the 'Victoria and Albert' steam yacht. Prince Albert was immediately rowed and pulled to shore. It is said that: 'the inhabitants of Babbacombe crowded the shore and every part of the hills to give expression to their feelings of loyalty'.

Prince Albert first visited The Glen and then enjoyed tea at the Cary Arms at which the royal party requested some Devonshire clotted cream. But to the dismay of the proprietor Mr Gasking, there was none available.

Thankfully help was at hand because Mrs Susan Ball and her friends were having a picnic tea and had plenty of cream. She immediately offered to share it with Prince Albert.

He then ascended through the shrubbery to the Downs and asked the way to St Marychurch in order to inspect the marble at Mr Woodley's marble showrooms. Prince Albert wanted to visit Mr Woodley because he had been awarded a gold medal for his circular marble inlaid table the year before at the Great Exhibition which Prince Albert must have been very impressed with.

On her visit to Babbacombe in 1846 Queen Victoria she wrote in her journal:

'Red cliffs and rocks with wooded hills like Italy... rocks and grottos with the deepest sea on which there was no ripple. We intended to disembark and walk up the hill, but it came on to rain very much.'

Her first visit to Babbacombe had been in 1833 when, as Princess Victoria she landed at Torquay Harbour and was brought to visit The Glen. How many places can boast that a monarch has visited the exact same spot three times?

Figure 64 – Afternoon tea at the thatched Cary Arms
(Torquay Museum Society Library)

Sir James and Lady Morrison also visited Mr Woodley's marble showrooms. In his holiday diary Sir James writes that on Friday 30 May 1851 they visited St Marychurch where: 'there are celebrated marble works' and Lady Morrison made a purchase of a candlestick as her holiday souvenir.

Mr Woodley's showrooms are on the left of Figure 65. The building still stands and is the Babbacombe Corinthian Yacht Club headquarters. Behind the showrooms were the actual marble works and the large house called Hillborough was Mr Woodley's home. You might recognise the site of Hillborough as being where the St Marychurch Coop supermarket stands in 2021.

On the right and over the wall is Hampton House and there is just a pedestrian access to it via a gate. The main entrance was as mentioned, at what is now the junction of Babbacombe Road and Babbacombe Downs Road and the house was reached via a long private driveway.

Figure 65 – Mr Woodley's showrooms and Hillborough his home
(Torquay Museum Society Library)

After their visit to the marble showroom, Sir James and Lady Morrison visited St Marychurch Church. He says that: 'the church is a conspicuous landmark at sea'. However, the church building in 1851 was not the one that exists today and in the mid-19th century the church was in an extremely bad state of repair. For example, the columns were ten inches out of perpendicular and the roof needed serious attention. So the church was rebuilt in 1861. Then the Norman tower (Figure 66) was taken down and rebuilt in 1871 as a memorial to Bishop Phillpotts, who had lived nearby at Bishopstowe, later to become the Palace Hotel. The hotel was demolished in 2020 and is to be rebuilt in a modern style.

Nearly a century after Sir James and Lady Morrison's visit, St Marychurch church was bombed and demolished on Sunday 30 May 1943 and tragically, 21 children and 3 Sunday school teachers were killed. The tower survived and the new 20th-century church was rebuilt alongside it in 1953. On the day of the bombing many men manhandled masonry and beams to retrieve the dead and the living.

I am now embarrassed to write about the part my fisherman grandfather Mark Badcott played in the rescue. The Vicarage Lodge cat had run up the damaged church tower. My grandfather and a friend climbed a ladder that they had placed against the church tower to try to grab the cat, but couldn't reach it. They then fetched someone the cat would trust, but still it would not come out, so my grandfather's friend asked him if he had a piece of fish in his pocket, which apparently he did and he tied a chunk to a stick and tempted the cat out. It was rescued.

Figure 66 – St Marychurch Church 1860 and Norman tower
(Torquay Museum Society Library)

We will now have a change of scenery with the impressions of 1857 St Marychurch and beyond, of eight-year-old Edmund Gosse. We will follow his excursion from his home at Sandhurst in St Marychurch Road up through Fore Street and down Park Road, and then another excursion when he visited Watcombe and Fore Street in Barton.

Edmund Gosse's father Philip was an extremely strict member of the very strict Plymouth Brethren denomination. Before Philip built the Fore Street chapel that became known as Gosse Chapel, the Plymouth Brethren worshipped somewhere, says Edmund, at the bottom of Park Road. Edmund had to attend chapel three times on a Sunday and hence walked to and fro three times. He reminisces and describes St Marychurch in 1857 in his book Father and Son which is the story of his childhood and relationship with his loving but austere father.

The village, at the southern end of Fore Street near to where their villa stood, was according to Edmund in 1857 not pretty. 'The foul smells which breathed on close days from the open doors and windows' made him feel faint. And there were horse droppings everywhere. He also tells us that Fore Street consisted of two parallel lines of houses, all whitewashed and most of them fronted by: 'trifling shop windows'.

The walk through Fore Street was very worrisome to him. He dreaded the rudeness of the children and walking on the inch or two of broken pavement in front of the houses was 'disagreeable and tiresome'. Many readers will probably remember Fore St with its very narrow pavements and the double decker buses going dangerously near to the buildings before the pedestrianisation in 1974.

Figure 67 – Fore St and Gosse Chapel (Image Terry Leaman)

Figure 68 - St Marychurch Church circa 1871 (Torquay Museum Society Library)

    The only handsome building in the village of St Marychurch was, according to Edmund, the ancient parish church with its shady churchyard. However, the church was he says almost entirely concealed by a variety of 'mean shops', which were demolished during his childhood in order to extend the graveyard. St Marychurch in 1857 is certainly different from what we might have expected and a complete contrast to the pleasant pedestrian shopping centre we enjoy today.

    Edmund then walked down Park Road towards the Plymouth Brethren meeting room and past the first house on the right-hand side in

Figure 69. It is one of the oldest in St Marychurch built circa 1800. There is even an archway leading to the back of the house where a horse might have been taken to a stable. The long terraces of Park Road were built between 1830 and 1860. So Edmund Gosse actually saw many of the same houses that we see today, but in his opinion it was a dreary street. What do you think?

I can understand where Edmund is coming from because as a boy I walked from home up and down this road for four years in the 1960s to Homelands Technical High School (now Spire Academy) and I can't remember anything particularly interesting. I do now of course enjoy its history.

For example, Park Crescent, just off Park Road in Cambridge Road is a recently renovated Grade II crescent of eight neo-Tudor style houses built circa 1840. Number 3 was the home of Isambard Kingdom Brunel's estate manager Alexander Forsyth between 1848 and 1851. The entrance to Number 1 is in Park Road just up from the circa 1800 cottage.

Figure 69 – Park Road and the circa 1800 house on the right

The little meeting place which Edmund had to walk to on a Sunday was called 'The Room' and was at the furthest extremity of 'dreary' Park Road. Edmund describes it as: 'a square empty room built for I know not what purpose, over a stable with ammoniac odours rising through the floor as we sat there at our long devotion'. 'The Room' might have been in one of the existing buildings that resemble old workshops or stables in Havelock Road (Figure 71) that ran parallel with the bottom section of Park Road, or a similar building in Stable Lane which is off Havelock Road.

Edmund also described several of the chapel folk and the following two caught my eye. The first was James Petheridge who was born before the French Revolution, so in 1857 he seemed extremely old to young Edmund and at least 69. He was tall and 'he wore on a Sunday, his full white smock, smartly embroidered down the front'. When he was sat says Edmund: 'he would raise the smock like a skirt and reveal his immensely long, thin legs, encased in tight leggings and finished off with shoes with buckles'. This must have been an astonishing sight to a boy who had just moved from London.

Another was Richard Moxhay a local stonemason. He was always dressed in a white corduroy suit: 'on which any stain of Devonshire mud was painfully conspicuous. When smartened up, his appearance suggested that somebody had given the suit a coating of whitewash which looked like Devonshire cream'.

Of course tastes, fashions and what constitutes one's 'Sunday best' have changed, but clearly the Sunday best of a man born towards the end of the 18th century was his white, embroidered smock or a white corduroy suit.

Figure 70 – Park Crescent

Figure 71 – Possible meeting room for the Plymouth Brethren in 1857

Edmund Gosse wasn't enamoured with St Marychurch, so what did he think of another part of the parish? He tells us that on a fine day he was taken for a walk by Mary Grace Burmington, a member of the chapel. Having walked down Park Road, they made their way to Pavor which is the area between Teignmouth Road and the Watcombe shopping centre. He tells us that in 1857 it was: 'almost decayed to extinction'. I wonder how dilapidated the buildings were? The modern photos of Holly Cottage in Figure 72 and Hockings Farm in Figure 73 that was owned from 1870 by my great-great uncle John Hockings certainly puts Pavor in a good light.

Edmund and Mary Grace then walked to Fore Street, Barton and to do so they had to walk through the sticky mud of the Pavor lanes. Barton was approached, says Edmund, along a deep lane which was all a wonder and a revelation to him. Just think about this. A few months before, this eight-year-old had been living in London and had never seen until this day any of our beautiful Devon lanes. A Midsummer's Night Dream Act II, Scene I describes the beauty and romance of an English lane:

> 'I know a bank where wild thyme blows,
> Where oxlips and the nodding violet grows,
> Quite over canopied with luscious woodbine,
> With sweet musk-roses and with eglantine.

Before World War II much of Watcombe and Barton resembled the landscape in Figure 74. It was predominantly a farming, quarrying and pottery community. There were at least two quarries. Lummaton Quarry was to the left of the postcard scene and Barton Quarry behind Fore Street is indicated by the red arrow. All had at least one lime kiln, and stone from Barton Quarry was used to build part of Torquay Town Hall. Watcombe Pottery was on the corner of Teignmouth Road and Pavor Road and very near to Hockings Farm (Figure 73). The rest was farmland. There were plentiful sources of water: the Barton Well, the Idewell and Stoney Wells and the River Fleete.

Before and after World War II a large swath of land was bought by the local authority to build much needed homes. The location that became my home at 8 Halsteads Road where I was born in 1952 is marked by the green arrow in Figure 74. Most of the old buildings were demolished and now just a few remain. For example, Dartmoor Lodge in Happaway Road, which is circled in red, is a limestone-walled bungalow that still exists. Many of the houses below Barton Quarry in Fore Street, Barton are still standing.

Figure 72 – Holly Cottage in Pavor, Watcombe   Figure 73 – Hockings Farm also in Pavor

Lummaton Quarry is geologically speaking one of the most important places in the world. In the early 19th century, scientists were working on a system for naming the main periods of geological time. Geologists found at Lummaton some unusual marine fossils they called the 'Lummaton Shell Beds' and declared that Lummaton was the most important single fossiliferous locality of that geological period in Britain and possibly the world. Following this research at Lummaton Quarry, the period of time 360 to 420 million years ago was named in 1840, after our own County of Devon, the 'Devonian Period'. The quarry is now an industrial estate and unaware of its scientific importance.

Figure 74 – Old Barton

After walking through the sticky mud of Pavor's lanes, Edmund then walked up Fore Street, Barton about which he was pleasantly surprised. And this is what he says: 'Barton has preserved its street of ancient detached cottages. Each had a garden which the inhabitants took pride in, with roses, jasmine and the stately cotoneaster which one sees nowhere at its best but in Devonshire cottage gardens. Barton was a vivid contrast to squalid St Marychurch and its absence of all vegetation'.

The Barton Conservation Appraisal written on behalf of Torbay Council in 2005 describes Fore Street and Church Road as an area of: 'walls, banks and hedges, and extensive tree cover. This provides a sense of enclosure and relative isolation from the later surrounding development. Several informally arranged cottage groups and short off-street spurs give the feel of an intricate village street'. There are also modern 20th-century houses, but this area of Torquay really does resemble a peaceful 19th-century time warp encircled by 20th-century housing estates.

From the junction of Clennon Lane and Fore Street there were and still are many notable buildings. The first one that Edmund Gosse might have spotted is situated down a side street and is the old Wesleyan Chapel. It was built between 1804 and 1806 and at the time was, with the exception of St Marychurch Church and Torre Church, the only place of worship in Torquay. Prior to its building the Methodist worshipers in Barton met in the parlour of Edward Henley after he and his brother John heard John Wesley preach in Exeter in the 1780s. There is a local legend that suggests that John Wesley preached in Barton Quarry, but alas, his diaries do not mention a visit to Barton or Torquay and the nearest town where he preached was Ashburton in 1766. However, there was a preaching circuit centred at Cullompton that extended to Torbay so it is possible that an itinerant preacher appointed by John Wesley did preach at the quarry. The Wesleyans expanded their work three years later by building another chapel in 1807 in Swan Street near Torquay Harbour. The Barton chapel closed a considerable time ago and has been converted into two houses.

Figure 75 – 1804 Wesleyan Chapel just off Fore Street, Barton
(Torquay Museum Society Library)

Walking up Fore Street Edmund Gosse would have walked past small terraces of 19th-century houses and a few larger houses. For example, on the left-hand side is the old Baptist Chapel. Its beginnings go back to a lease dated 27 July 1779 and 5 April 1794 when the gathering was first known as the 'Calvinist Meeting House' occupied by a 'Body of Protestant Dissenters of the Particular or Calvinist Baptist Denomination'.

On 13 March 1830 twelve trustees were appointed under the leadership of Charles Troward of Paignton who was a 'Gentleman'. He and the other eleven are listed in an interesting document dated 5 June 1868 that also records the names of the current and newly appointed trustees of that year. The Chapel building commenced after 13 March 1830 and it was opened for worship in 1831. An early minister was Mr Daw who lived at Prospect Cottage situated near to Barton Cross.

Whilst other Torquay Baptists had met together for some years in Swan Street near Torquay Harbour, it was not formally constituted into a church until 4 January 1832, making Barton Baptist Chapel the oldest Baptist place of worship in the town by two years.

In 1868 the trustees included the Rev Evan Edwards, the minister of Upton Vale Baptist Church, and this commenced the long association of the mother church of Barton Chapel with its now much larger offspring in Torquay town centre overseeing its activities.

Figure 76 – The Old Baptist Church
(Cliff Howle collection)

Two of the original trustees were living abroad: Charles Troward was now living in America, and the Coffinswell butcher, John Osborn, was living in Natal, South Africa. Surprisingly, it seems that both continued as trustees.

The Trustees of Barton Baptist Chapel on 13 March 1830

Charles Troward of Paignton, Gentleman
Nathaniel Pearce of Stokeinteignhead, Yeoman
Thomas Pitts Hannaford of St Marychurch, Cooper
Samuel Henley Taylor of St Marychurch, Builder
James Walling of St Marychurch, Carpenter
James Staddon of St Marychurch, Yeoman
William Bowden Senior of St Marychurch, Yeoman
William Bowden Junior of St Marychurch, Yeoman
John Terry of St Marychurch, Carpenter and Joiner
John Toms of Shaldon, Tailor
Samuel Langmead of Ringmore, Basket Maker
John Osborn of Coffinswell, Butcher

The Trustees of Barton Baptist Chapel on 5 June 1868

Old continuing Trustees
Charles Troward now in America, Gentleman
William Bowden now in Coffinswell, Yeoman
John Toms of Shaldon, Tailor
John Osborn now in Natal, South Africa, Butcher

Newly appointed Trustees
William Hall Senior of St Marychurch, Yeoman
William Hall Junior of St Marychurch, Yeoman
John Hall of St Marychurch, Gentleman
Robert Ellis Hall of Crediton, School Master
William Wills Bowden of Coffinswell, Yeoman
Joseph Aggett of Newton Abbot, Gentleman
Evan Edwards of Torquay, Baptist Minister
James Walling of St Marychurch, Builder

The Baptist Chapel survived until 1946 when a bungalow in Happaway Road was bought and converted into a church to serve the growing population in Barton. By then the houses in Barton Hill Road and Isaacs Road had been erected and a new estate of local authority housing was about to built on the fields of Clennon Farm and would become Halstead's Road and Falloway Close. The old Chapel was sold in 1950 and became a private residence.

Further up on the right-hand side behind a 20th-century house is a now inaccessible lime kiln and further up again is 155 Fore Street which is the beautifully kept 18th-century, thatched Lea Cottage. Previous owners were Brian and Carole Cresswell who were respected members of the Torquay Museum Society. Next door is a slate-roofed circa 1850 cottage that was once a shop, run by M & H Jones and at one time it was a haberdashery. The shop sign can still be seen over what was the shop window.

Figure 77 – The old Baptist Chapel built circa 1831

**Figure 78 – circa 1910 just a few houses behind the Baptist Chapel
(Cliff Howle collection)**

Carole Cresswell has provided some facts and figures about Lea Cottage. Although the earliest documents were dated in the 1800s, it was built in the 18th century and used to be two cottages. In fact the two thatched porches still exist (Figure 81) and a downstairs room has the shape of a doorway where the now redundant and demolished second staircase was situated. Two internal doors are thought to be original.

Figure 79 – The Baptist Chapel is on the left and thatched Lea Cottage further up on the right (Cliff Howle collection)

Figure 80 – 18C Lea Cottage adjoined to a 19C cottage
Figure 81 – the two front doors of Lea Cottage (Image Carole Cresswell)

Lea Cottage also has a bricked-up doorway that at one time connected it with the adjoining 153 Fore Street and together probably formed part of a farm complex. 153 Fore Street would have been merely a hay loft, and next to it an old smithy. On the deeds of Lea Cottage is a small line leading to the end of the back garden. On the other side of the garden wall in a neighbouring property there was what seemed to be a path through the undergrowth. After a storm this undergrowth blew over and revealed a set of steps carved out of the rock leading to a path. Many years ago a previous owner of Lea Cottage found a man in his back garden who said he was using an ancient public right of way. An explanation could be that prior to the closure of Barton Quarry behind Fore Street, the current public path from Moor Lane Close through to Wesley Close ran from Moor Lane and past the front doors of Lea Cottage to Fore St.

On the higher side of Lea Cottage was another thatched cottage (Figure 82) that caught fire in the 1940s. A house in nearby Isaacs Road was bombed and sparks from that burning house set the thatched cottage alight and it was destroyed.

Figure 82 – Fore St Barton (Image Carole Cresswell)

Further up from Lea Cottage, Edmund Gosse could have turned right, walked along Church Road and would have come across more fascinating buildings. At the far end is the 18th-century thatched Lavender Cottage (Figure 83). Then there is the terrace of workers homes called Tor Hill Cottages (Figure 84) which were erected in 18th and 19th centuries.

Half way along Church Road is the old St Augustine's combined school and chapel designed by Isambard Kingdom Brunel but built after his death by his wife and sons circa 1878. It became redundant in 1939 when St Martin's Church in Barton Hill Road was consecrated. St Augustine's has since been converted into two dwellings (Figure 85). Brunel had planned to erect ten workers cottages near to the site of St Augustine's. He built just four in 1852 which were very new in Edmund Gosse's time and he does not comment on them. The other six houses were never built. The four which are in Barn Close have been extensively modernised and upgraded but are a testament to Brunel's desire to provide homes, a chapel and a school for his estate workers and their families.

Figure 83 – 18C Lavender Cottage

Figure 84 – 18C and 19C Tor Hill Cottages

Figure 85 – St Augustine's Chapel and School, now two dwellings

At the very top of Fore Street is what I refer to as the secret part of Barton. This final stretch of the road is now a cul-de-sac and the 16th-century Manor House is only seen by those on foot. It is another beautifully kept building and has been converted into two residences. The old Manor House was at first a 16th-century open-hall farmhouse. In the 17th century additional floors were added and the house has continued to evolve over the centuries. The outbuildings have been converted into further accommodation.

Further on from Fore Street is the road to Barton Cross where Edmund visited Miss Daw, the daughter of the minister of the Baptist Chapel. They lived at Prospect Cottage which he describes as: 'a solitary little house high up at Barton Cross'. This early 19th-century house still exists but now of course it is surrounded by 20th-century homes.

Edmund loved his visits to Miss Daw because she always excitedly took him to the place that he loved most – the summer house - where he could see what he loved most: the sea and the distant waters of Tor Bay.

Yes! The sea, always the sea, nothing but the sea. The summer house had a table encrusted with cowry shells on which Miss Daw served up Devonshire cream and small, hard biscuits that he says were like pebbles. Edmund quotes an anonymous poet that might sum up how many of us feel about a view of the sea. Perhaps Miss Daw recited it to him:

> 'In the downhill of life, when I find I'm declining,
> May my lot no less fortunate be
> Than a snug elbow chair can afford for reclining,
> And a cot that o'erlooks the wide sea.'

Figure 86 – 16C Manor House

Beyond Barton Cross there existed, says Edmund, a fairyland: 'All was mysterious, unexplored and rich with infinite possibilities'. I experienced just that when I was 7 or 8 years old in the late 1950s. A family friend, Miss Hilda Maddock, who lived in Cambridge Road took my twin sister Anne, me and other children up to Barton Cross, Great Hill and Rocombe where we picked what seemed like hundreds of primroses from the hedge banks of Devon's glorious lanes. It still is an incredibly beautiful part of rural South Devon.

Figure 87 – Prospect Cottage in 2020

Farther on from Barton Cross and a ten minute walk away is Great Hill, Torquay's highest point at 180 metres above sea level and it has tremendous views of St Marychurch and Tor Bay. The spire and tower of the two churches in particular stand out (and can be seen from as far away as Haytor Rocks twenty miles away on Dartmoor).

Great Hill came into public ownership in 1911 when the owner of the Brunel Estate, Colonel Ichabod Wright, sold up. Torquay Council was able to buy Great Hill and the surrounding six acres for £270 for 'waterworks and other public purposes'. The Great Hill reservoir was built, but just as importantly the public footpaths gave access to the glorious views.

Figure 88 – A view of St Marychurch from Great Hill

From Great Hill there are footpaths and lanes to Maidencombe which, whilst it is in the parish of Stokeinteignhead, is within the boundary of Torbay Council and hence I've taken the liberty of including it in this chapter. It is at Maidencombe where in 1842 we will meet up with Matthew Bridges who is on holiday and he has walked the coastline from Torquay to Maidencombe, passing through Babbacombe and Watcombe. Arriving at Maidencombe, the scene greeting him would have been very similar to what we see in 2021. This old area of the village near the cliffs and beach can still be reached by the coast path from Torquay or via Brim Hill, Rock House Lane and Steep Hill. It retains, like Fore Street in Barton, a sense of tranquility and rural beauty and a feeling of remoteness.

There is a cluster of five old thatched cottages including the 16th-century Court House and a few other houses around the popular and, in my opinion, still unspoilt Thatched Tavern. It was once the Bungalow Tea Gardens and extremely popular. Unfortunately though, on 6 September 2019 a fire broke out in the kitchen which caused severe damage to half of the ground floor. Thankfully, there were no casualties. The tavern has since been sold and fortunately it has reopened and the garden remains what it has been for decades - a peaceful spot for a cool drink on a hot summer's day.

The substantial 16th-century thatched Court House is on the site of an earlier Manor House that may date back to the 14th century. In its garden is an equally ancient Judas Tree which is thought to have been brought back from the Lebanon in the 16th century. Many years ago the tree became partially uprooted but, on a visit to it in 2020, it was still alive and well and in good leaf. It is such an important tree that there is a plaque nearby with the words: 'Cercis Siliquastrum (Judas Tree) preserved as a tree of special interest by Torquay Borough Council'. It produces beautiful red flowers in springtime and has its name through the myth that Judas Iscariot hanged himself from a tree of this species causing its white flowers to turn red.

Between the two World Wars camping in Maidencombe became very popular in the summer and in 1938 the Torquay Borough Council compulsorily purchased many fields in the locality in an attempt to curtail this. Then, in more recent times, there was a proposal to build homes opposite the beautiful thatched buildings and to the relief of residents this application was turned down. This same area is now designated a green space and is under the care of the Torbay Coast and Countryside Trust.

However, the 21st century has caught up with remote Maidencombe. Behind the thatched cottage to the left of the Thatched Tavern is a new building delightfully called Oystercatcher Court and is according to the estate agent's information board: 'a select development of 1 and 2 bed apartments'. It sits on the footprint of a previous building but, is in my opinion, overwhelmingly big and out of character with its neighbours.

The South Devon coastline and its scenery inspired Matthew Bridges to write an evocative poem about the coastal fringes of 19th-century St Marychurch and it includes verses from Ilsham all the way to Maidencombe. Here is his verse about Maidencombe:

> 'Lead me still further on, where seamews call
> From their lone watches o'er the Maiden's Fall.
> That stream of foam, descending night and day,
> Upon the barren beach in showers of spray.'

After admiring the quaint and quiet lanes and buildings of Maidencombe, Matthew Bridges walked down the steep paths and steps to its beach. He mentions a waterfall and until I read this poem some years ago, I was unaware of one being there. It had poured over the cliff to the beach for centuries, maybe even for millennia, until the early 1970s when the local council, no doubt on health and safety grounds, piped it and it was forgotten by most, but not for the residents of Maidencombe. After periods of heavy rain the pipe often becomes blocked and the waterfall retakes it ancient route over the cliff. One year in exceptionally wet and cold weather it actually froze. I think it is a shame that a beautiful natural feature such as a waterfall and what could be a geological asset to the beach and area has been deliberately hidden from view. Matthew Bridges uses the word seamew in his poem which is an old name for a seagull.

Figure 89 – The Bungalow Tea Gardens, now the Thatched Tavern

Figure 90 – Beach approach and Maiden's Fall at Maidencombe Beach circa 1911

We will now leave Maidencombe, its thatched cottages and waterfall and follow the coast path from Maidencombe to Watcombe Beach with Matthew Bridges as he retraces his steps. His four poetic lines about mid 19th-century Watcombe will be our guide:

> Lead me to Watcombe — where the waves are rolled
> Round rocks of wonder — rifted — bare — and bold.
> Where the sly otter steals ashore uncurbed,
> And ravens croak in echoes undisturbed.

First, we head down to Watcombe Beach where I just love the way the crystal clear water's edge is in an arc and is surrounded by wooded conglomerate sandstone cliffs. Despite the landslide and cliff falls in February 2020 it is still possible to get to the beach and it remains a great place to spend a peaceful hour or so. But what did Watcombe Beach look like when Matthew Bridges visited it in 1842? What did he see when he walked down the steep descent to the beach? This 1830 print (Figure 93) is unmistakably Watcombe Beach. There are fishing boats and the fishermen are boiling up bark and water in a pot to create creosote, dipping their cotton or hemp nets into this pot of preservative and then hanging them out to dry. It's an ancient process called 'barking'.

Matthew Bridges mentions in his poem the sea otters at Watcombe Beach, but they have long since disappeared. He also mentions: 'rocks of wonder — rifted — bare — and bold'. Was he referring to the rocks on the beach? He might have been, but more than likely he was describing Watcombe's Valley of the Rocks.

The 'Torquay Directory' newspaper described the valley as a natural amphitheatre formed in remote ages by a gigantic landslip. On its northern side stands: 'a towering precipice of conglomerate fissured by the storms of far more centuries than ever looked down upon the pyramids'. The newspaper is describing the Giant Rock.

The Valley of the Rocks is on the coast path between Watcombe Beach and Maidencombe. To get there walk just 30 yards from Watcombe Beach car park, which is situated where the horse is standing in Figure 94, along the coast path and look up. Through the trees you will see the 150 foot high Giant Rock of sandstone conglomerate. Until the end of the 19th century, the area was grazed and treeless, but when grazing stopped the area reverted to its natural woodland state. That is why the scenes in Figures 94 and 95 are almost unrecognisable as the area we know today. A little farther on towards Maidencombe is Goats' Path, clinging to the side of the hill and it is still part of the coast path leading eventually to Maidencombe.

Figure 91 – Watcombe Beach 2019

Figure 92 – Watcombe Beach 2019

Figure 93 – Watcombe Beach circa 1830 (Torquay Museum Society Library)

On the 28 July 1852 and the 1 September 1853 an extraordinary event took place in the Valley of the Rocks. It was the 'musical fete champetre' organised by the Torquay Choral Society. The 1852 fete was a resounding success and the 1853 event would be even grander. The 'Torquay Directory' newspaper tells us that 8,000 people attended the 1853 event including those who came by train from Birmingham and London and were then ferried from Torquay Harbour to Watcombe Beach by steamer. Those attending included: 'not only the elite but also a vast assemblage of all classes from the immediate neighbourhood'. Members of the Imperial Russian family attended including Her Imperial Highness the Princess Olga and the Crown Prince of Wurttemberg.

Figure 94 –Giant Rock in the Valley of the Rocks, Watcombe

Figure 95 – The Goats' Path is in the distance on the right of the picture

The musical fete champetre was a garden party on a grand scale. The band of the Royal Marines and the Torquay Subscription Band stood below the 150 foot high Giant Rock, playing away. And a 100-strong choir from the Plymouth Philharmonic and Torquay Choral Society sang madrigals (unaccompanied choir pieces) and glees (songs for men's voices in three or more parts, usually unaccompanied). It must have been an awesome sound in that natural amphitheatre.

There was a maypole around which children dressed in white and wearing wreaths of flowers on their heads danced, weaving their varied coloured garlands around the pole. I remember dancing around the maypole on Babbacombe Downs when I was at primary school around 1960.

During the afternoon break, cake, teas and Devonshire cream, were served in a marquee under the direction of Mrs Griffiths. And in the evening there was a most brilliant illumination of the Giant Rock producing an exceedingly grand appearance and the entertainment was rounded off by the singing of the national anthem.

There were however downsides to the fete. There was a 'splendid balloon' which as it was being inflated broke from its moorings and was destroyed. And there was the daunting task of organising toilet facilities for 8,000 people in an out-of-the-way place. How did they do that? The biggest concern was that scarcely one-third paid for admission to the fete, with even 'many of the well-dressed' avoiding payment. And the consequence? The musical fete champetre was never held at the Valley of the Rocks again.

The next beach south of Watcombe Beach and the Valley of the Rocks is Petit Tor Beach and in 1853 Philip Gosse wrote a fascinating description of it. Prior to the Gosse family moving to St Marychurch in 1857, they had spent a few months in the St Marychurch area in 1853. Philip must have been so taken with the locality that he decided that the village must become his new home. As a marine biologist the area had so much for him to study and he was also able to perfect his invention of the marine aquarium with an endless supply of sea creatures and plants.

The downhill walk to Petit Tor Beach in 2021 is via Petit Tor Downs and a muddy path through the woods. In 1853 it was very different. Philip Gosse writes:

'On the February 3rd 1853 I walked down to the cove at Petit Tor. A zigzag road leads down to the beach through the gulley which bears the name of Petit Tor where Mr Woodley cuts the great blocks of variegated marble which he makes into his well-known tables and chimney pieces. Huge blocks of marble were lying beside the way at different points ready for removal. At the cove there are the ruined walls of what was once probably a fisherman's cottage built of rough fragments of friable limestone set in a strong red mortar. In the midst of the beach there is a columnar mass of rough conglomerate rock about 60 feet high.'

Figure 96 – Petit Tor Beach circa 1828 and the column called Lot's Wife (Torquay Museum Society Lib

Figure 97 – Petit Tor Beach circa 1906

By 1906 'Lot's Wife', the column of rock mentioned by Philip Gosse, had been badly eroded (Figure 97) and by the middle of the 20th century it had disappeared. The ruins of the cottage had completely disappeared too. Neither is there a zigzag road to the beach and that too has gone as has the marble quarry. The beach is only reached by that steep and muddy path of red earth which is so abundant says Philip Gosse that: 'it tinges the clothes of the peasants, the coats of the numerous donkeys, and the wool of the sheep'.

The Petit Tor marble quarry was a huge enterprise. Mr Woodley's marble was used to make the souvenirs bought by the likes of Lady Morrison from his St Marychurch showroom and the furniture admired by Prince Albert. However, the marble was also transported by sea and used to construct the beautiful columns and pillars for many churches. St John's Church situated above Torquay Harbour now a Grade I listed building, is a wonderful local example.

As a teenager, my friends and I in the late 1960s and early 1970s would often go to Petit Tor Beach for a BBQ and a swim, but the beach is now frequented by naturists and considered out-of-bounds by many, myself included. Had Philip Gosse, the naturalist and leader of a Plymouth Brethren chapel known that the beach would become one for naturists he would, I think, have been rather disappointed.

Figure 98 has two views of the quarry and beach in 2021. The left-hand photo is looking down to the beach from the cliff edge that is near to the triangulation pillar on Petit Tor, 350 feet above the sea. Just up from the beach is a quantity of grey quarry spoil and in the undergrowth lays a pulley wheel from a quarry winch that moved who knows how many tons of marble. The old track to the quarry was from Petitor Downs and through the gully in the right hand photo.

Figure 98 – Petit Tor Quarry 2020

Just around the corner from Petit Tor Beach is the ever-popular Oddicombe Beach and was visited by Sir James and Lady Morrison in 1851. Above the beach says Sir James is: 'the lofty down of Babbicombe' and he and Lady Morrison 'overlooked a precipice from whence you see the shore and its beautiful emerald green waves' (Figure 99). Now the waves are sometimes a reddish brown, coloured by the sandstone and red clay brought down by the 2010 and 2013 landslides.

Sir James describes the path down to Oddicombe Beach (there was no road yet) and the beach itself. He wrote that he and his wife: 'walked down a steep and rugged path and strolled and strolled along the beach picking up pebbles and shells - and there were boats and fishermen mending their nets'. And after buying a crab for a few coppers they made their way back up the path. It's a real insight into life in the mid-19th century at Oddicombe Beach.

Figure 99 – Oddicombe Beach circa 1906 (TuckDB postcard)

At the beginning of this chapter we read the words: 'the sea, always the sea, nothing but the sea' which were written by Sir Edmund Gosse describing his feelings about Babbacombe Bay as a boy. Edmund also describes his first visit in 1857 to Babbacombe Downs from his home in St Marychurch Road. This is what he wrote:

'How my heart remembers! We hastened along a couple of high walled lanes, when suddenly, far below us, in an immense arc of light, there stretched the enormous plain of waters. We had but to cross a step or two of Downs, when the hollow sides of that great cove - Oddicombe Beach - yawned at our feet, descending, like a broken cup, down, down to the moon of snow white shingle and the expanse of blue-green sea.'

To reach the Downs, Edmund had walked past the high walls of Hampton House and he probably looked over the same precipice as Sir James Morrison. Babbacombe Downs had no fencing, no seats and no footpaths. It was still an open area of grass, gorse and bracken, and used to graze sheep and goats. It resembled the terrain of early 21st-century Wall's Hill, but without the wire fence. Edmund describes the beach at Oddicombe as 'snow white shingle'. That too has gone although as recent as the 1960s the beach was one of large pebbles. Since then, the tide and storms, the sandstone and the clay from the rock falls have changed Oddicombe Beach to a grainy terracotta-coloured sandy beach.

Philip Gosse writing in 1853 explains that he too made his way along a slippery path at Babbacombe Downs and came to the edge of an abrupt perpendicular cliff. He however, decided it was safer to get to Oddicombe by walking down to Babbacombe Beach from where he climbed along 'the beautiful arc of alternate rock and shingle' at low tide to Oddicombe.

Before the sea defences of large boulders were built between Oddicombe and Babbacombe beaches it was still possible at low tide to walk between the two. Philip Gosse scrambled and waded across the rocks shown in Figure 101. I did this many times in the 1960s and I learnt to dive from one of those rocks at high tide.

Philip Gosse discovered on his first afternoon at Oddicombe Beach a feature that no longer exists. He found there a circular rock pool about 3 feet wide and 3 feet deep, full of pure sea water, quite still, and clear as crystal. It was full of beautiful delicate seaweeds and he discovered two previously unknown sea anemones: Sagartia nivea and Sagartia rosea. In the 1850s all the rock pools were literally teeming with fish, crabs, molluscs and plants.

Figure 100 – Oddicombe Beach 1912

Philip would on his visits to Oddicombe and other beaches take samples home, keep them in his sea aquarium and produce the most amazing paintings of them which were published in his many books. The popularity of his books produced an army of rock pool collectors who, by the first decade of the 20th century, had destroyed what had existed for centuries. It's ironic and tragic that Philip Gosse the marine zoologist, who was so religious and reverent, was inadvertently responsible for the demise of the abundant rock pools - a calamity that he had never anticipated.

Figure 101 – low tide between Babbacombe and Oddicombe Beaches circa 1930

Edmund Gosse also relates how he and his father were always on the local beaches looking for and into rock pools and Edmund tells us that his father always wore black clothes including an enormous black felt hat even on a trip to the seaside.

Figure 102 – A Philip Gosse painting from *Actinologia Britannica*

From Babbacombe Downs it is just a ten-minute walk to the triangular shaped Wall's Hill that gives a feel for what Babbacombe Downs used to be like. It's covered in coarse grass, bracken, gorse and blackberry bushes. On two sides of this triangle are dramatic 85 metre high cliffs and on its southern side there is a striking view of nearby Anstey's Cove from where there is a fine view of Wall's Hill and Long Quarry.

Philip Gosse writes that at Long Quarry ships of considerable size moored at a natural pier and were loaded with blocks of limestone. He asked a quarry man – maybe it was my great-great grandfather Francis Eales - if there was any practical way down to Long Quarry. He was told that there was just a narrow and precarious path from Wall's Hill to be used only by experienced stone workers. He was also told about a quarryman: 'who was lately dashed to pieces by falling from near the site although he had been nearly 50 years in the occupation'. That narrow and precarious path still is, in 2021, the only way down to the now deserted quarry.

He also describes one of his many visits to Anstey's Cove. The walk down was via steps and crooked paths and not dissimilar to the steep walk down in 2021, except that now there is also a narrow private road for service vehicles. The path, says Philip is: 'tangled with briers and ferns; where the swelling buds of the hawthorn and honeysuckle are already bursting and where the blackbird mellowly whistles in the fast-greening thicket'. He continues:

> 'Yonder on the shingle lies a boat, newly painted in white and green, for the attraction of young ladies of maritime aspirations; she is hauled up high and dry; but the sinewy arms of honest Harry Bate, who hearing footsteps has come out of his little grotto under the rock to reconnoitre, will soon drag her down to the rippling waves, and, "for the small sum of a shilling an hour," will pull us over the smooth and pond-like sea, whithersoever we may choose to direct him. "Jump aboard, please, Sir! Jump in, ladies! Jump in, little master!" And now, as we take our seats on the clean canvas cushions astern, the boat's bottom scrapes along with a harsh grating noise over the white shingle-pebbles, and we are afloat.'

Even in the 1850s tourists could hire a boatman and take a boat ride. The tradition continued for well over 100 years at Anstey's Cove and the adjacent Redgate Beach. In the 1920s and 1930s passengers embarked and disembarked from the 'Lorna Doone' whilst after World War II the pleasure boats 'White Heather', 'Nomad' and 'Seacrest' skippered at different times by my father, Raymond Badcott, sailed in and out of Redgate Beach (Figure 103). Rowing boats were also available for hire as were 'floats' which were the forerunners of the modern paddleboards and sea kayaks.

The old cliff path from Wall's Hill down to Redgate Beach was closed owing to rock falls around 1998 and Redgate Beach itself was closed around 2005 when the beach was deemed unsafe after further rock falls. But thankfully the tradition of hiring water craft continues at Anstey's Cove where sea kayaks and paddleboards are available for hire from Jeff and Lucy Stokes, the cafe proprietors.

And like Oddicombe Beach, Anstey's Cove was in the 1850s a 'white shingle beach' which is clearly visible in a circa 1936 photo (Figure 104) of my father, Raymond, and my grandfather, Mark Badcott, who was a Babbacombe fisherman and whose fishing nets were just offshore. In 2021 the beach is a mixture of sand, pebbles and boulders of various sizes. It seems that after the promenade was built in the years after World War II, the shingle was dragged out to sea by tides and storms and the level of the beach dropped.

Nelson's 'Torquay and Neighbourhood' published in 1867 describes Anstey's Cove as: 'one of the loveliest spots in the neighbourhood and it is difficult to describe without employing language which to the reader will seem that of exaggeration'. In my opinion too, Anstey's Cove really is that special. If you have not yet ventured down the steep descent to it, I highly recommend that you do.

Above – Raymond Badcott (Skipper) and Basil Dunstan (Deck Hand)
Top right – Mark Badcott on the bow
Bottom Right – Harry Wheaton on the bow

Figure 103 – The pleasure boats at Anstey's Cove and Redgate Beach

Figure 105 was taken on a warm August evening in 2016 at the beach party celebrating the 10th anniversary of the reopening of the beach café by Jeff and Lucy Stokes. As we sat there, a late 19th-century Brixham trawler 'The Pilgrim' sailed into the bay and my mind turned to Edmund Gosse's moving poem written in 1908. He had moved to London when he was a young man for employment and returned to Torquay and Anstey's Cove many times:

> The breeze inscribes with ring on ring,
> The grizzled oily seas of spring.
> Around the headland, gray and pale
> Comes like a ghost, a gliding sail.
> Through brooding tides I see her come,
> Where once I rowed where once I swum.
> Ah! Then that weltering water's hue
> Was rainbow purple, peacock blue.

> She veers & fades, she dies away
> In gulfs of universal gray,
> And of my boyhood and its boasts
> She seems the melancholy ghost.

Figure 104 – Anstey's Cove circa 1936. Mark Badcott right & Raymond Badcott centre

We are almost at the end of our day out in the mid-19th-century parish of St Marychurch and in the words of Matthew Bridges we are returning to our starting point of Babbacombe:

> Then bear me back to whence this theme began
> To Nature's sweetest scenes for mortal man,
> That peaceful hamlet seated on the sea,
> Dear to Devonia — memory — and me.

The parish of St Marychurch had revitalised Matthew Bridges. Before his visit, his poetry suggested a man who was depressed. However, after his holiday he wrote his brightest poetry and most inspiring hymns. After the death of his first wife, the St Marychurch air must have had a strange effect on him, because he remarried a lady 28 years younger than himself, and he lived to the ripe old age of 94.

I'm now wondering what part of this old parish has revitalised you and if you have your own favourite place. Maybe it's that peaceful 19th-century time warp called Fore Street in Barton, perhaps it's the mysterious sounding Valley of the Rocks at Watcombe, or Anstey's Cove described as one of the loveliest spots in the neighbourhood. Matthew Bridges loved Babbacombe and called it his hamlet of peace. Here are more lines from his poem that speak for themselves:

Hamlet of peace, — to me of all most sweet,
A zigzag road for vulgar wheels too steep,
Where the choice charms of earth and ocean,
Where only lovers ever learn to leap - meet.
The rocks so tall, and yet so full of flowers.

That glassy sea - outspread from morn till even,
The mirror of a blue and cloudless heaven,
Whilst cloven crags and marble quarries fair
Surround the calm, and shine reflected there.

Figure 105 – From Anstey's Cove August 2016 (Photo Rowena Coote)

Figure 106 – Anstey's Cove 2016 (Photo Rowena Coote)

I hope you have enjoyed your day out. It has been a whistle stop tour because there was so much to see and to be said about this fascinating part of Torquay. And whatever is thought of the seemingly unstoppable 21st-century changes to Babbacombe and St Marychurch, I hope that like me you still consider it as a peaceful hamlet seated on the sea.

CHAPTER 5

FOLLOWING TORQUAY'S RIVER FLEETE

Torquay is built some say, on seven hills from where there are beautiful views of the sea, the countryside and the moors. It has beaches and coves of sand and shingle with headlands jutting towards the sea. But it does not have a large river flowing through it. There is no River Dart or River Teign. Torquay does however have its tiny and forgotten River Fleete and following it from its source to the sea – a journey of about three miles - will reveal much about the history of Torquay.

The River Fleete rises somewhere in Watcombe or on higher ground towards Great Hill. For example a stream that runs beneath the 16th-century Old Manor House at the top of Fore Street, Barton may be its source. The 1939 OS map shows its source being in Mincent Hill, but no one knows for sure, because its source has been covered for some time. The first glimpse of the river is in the middle of the Firlands Road Green (Figure 109).

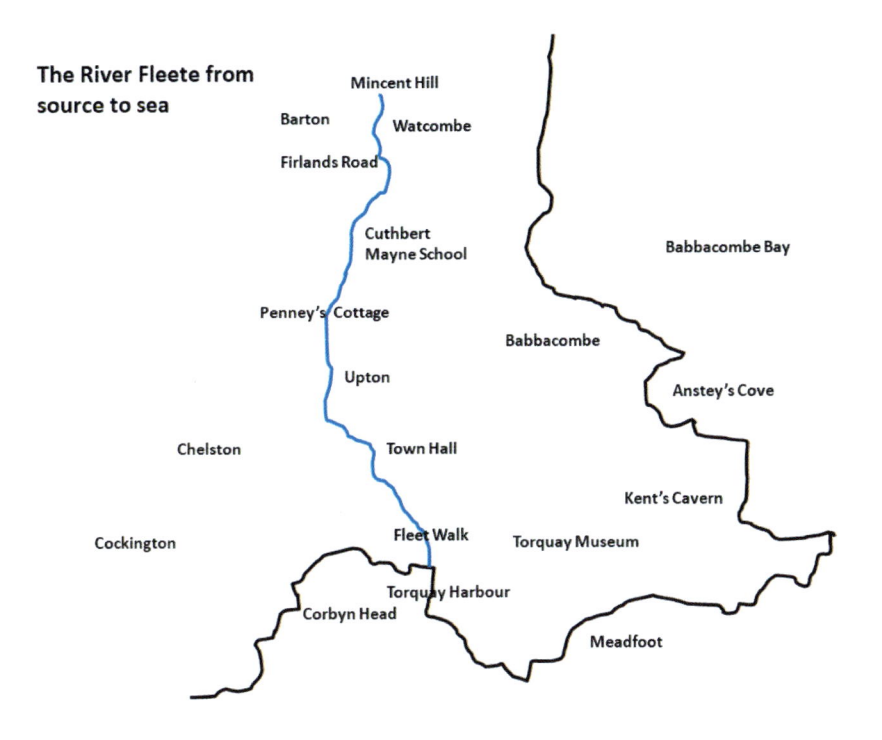

Before World War II much of the Torquay suburbs of Watcombe and Barton resembled the landscape in Figure 107. It was predominantly a farming, quarrying and pottery community. There were two quarries. Lummaton Quarry is marked on the 1939 OS map (Figure 108) and was to the left of the scene in Figure 107 and Barton Quarry is indicated by the red arrow. Both quarries had a lime kiln. Watcombe Pottery was behind Fore Street and Pavor Road, and called the 'Art Potteries' in the 1939 OS map. The rest was farmland. There were plentiful sources of water: the Barton Well, Idewell, Stoney Well and the River Fleete.

Before and after World War II a large swath of land in Barton and Watcombe enclosed within the red line in Figure 108 was bought by the local authority to build much-needed homes. The location that became my home at 8 Halsteads Road, where I was born in 1952, is marked by the green arrow in Figure 107 and Firlands Road where the River Fleete is first seen is marked by the yellow arrow.

Figure 107 – Old Barton

You might be disappointed at the width and flow of Torquay's river. In recent times it has never been more than a babbling brook, although the size of the old bridges it passed under suggests that it must have been a much larger stream.

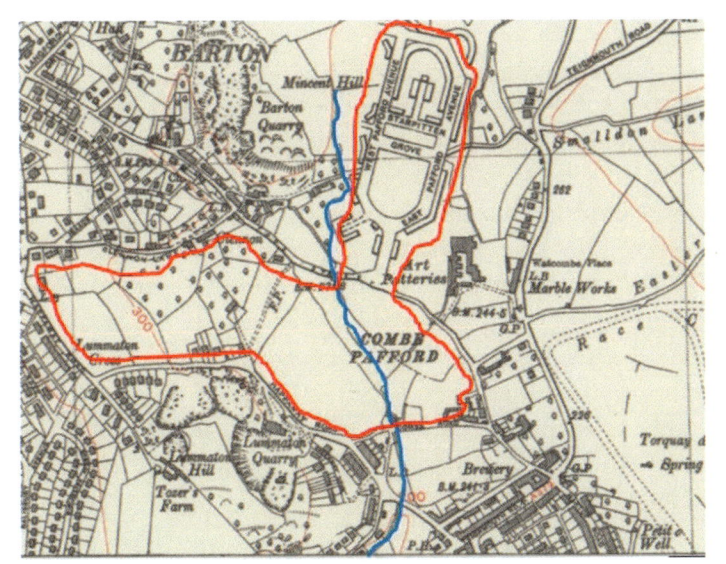

Figure 108 - The River Fleete from Mincent Hill to Coombe Lane marked in blue
(Reproduced with the permission of the National Library of Scotland)

Figure 109 – The River Fleete running through the centre of Firlands Road Green

The river flows from Firlands Road to the sea in the valley between Coombe Lane and Teignmouth Road, then piped and unseen it continues under Teignmouth Road, past Penney's Cottage and Stantaway Hill, along Lymington Road to Castle Circus, down through Union Street and Fleet Walk to the harbour.

From Firlands Road the Fleete runs underground for about 50 yards and passes under Combe Road. It then reappears and flows parallel to Coombe Lane for about 500 yards. Firstly behind six houses between Combe Road and Happaway Road where another small stream from behind Lummaton Place joins it. The river itself cannot be seen because of overgrown brambles and other vegetation, but it can be heard.

Before the six 1970s houses were built on this patch of land it was a scrubby field where, as a boy, I loved to visit the Shire horse that was kept in it. And when aged 11 to 14, I would walk past this spot every weekday on my way to and from school in Plainmoor.

The Fleete now passes under Happaway Road from where another glimpse of it can be seen looking down into a back garden of Coombe Lane. It then flows out of sight along the back of the gardens of nine houses in Coombe Lane, including the little known thatched cottage (Figure 111) and its garden in Figure 112. Behind these nine back gardens is the Coombe Lane playing field that was once called William's Field.

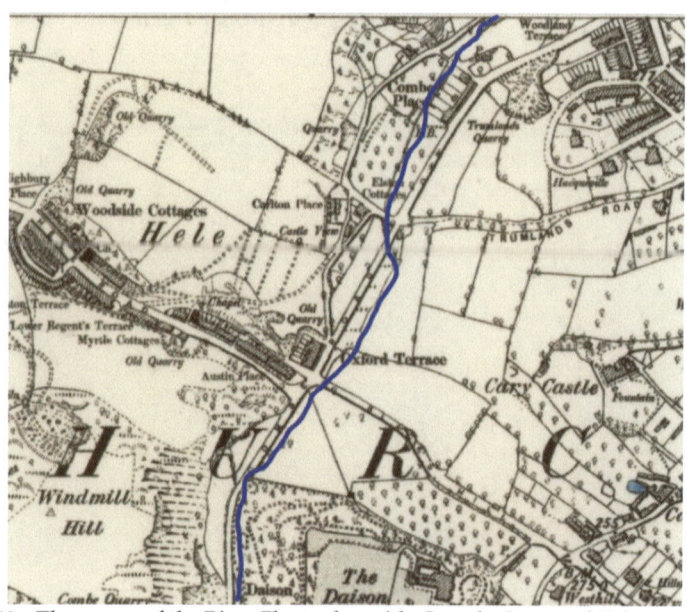

Figure 110 – The course of the River Fleete alongside Coombe Lane and Teignmouth Road in 1889 (Reproduced with the permission of the National Library of Scotland)

At the downstream end of the playing field there is surprisingly, an electricity sub-station on what the authorities say is a flood plain. There is a brief view of the river at an unnamed lane at the entrance to the playing field where it flows under this lane and continues between Teignmouth Road and Coombe Lane.

At the lane on a hot May afternoon in 2020 there was a tiny stream of water (Figure 113). However, 50 yards further on, that trickle had disappeared at what appears to be an ancient arched bridge in Combe Place (Figure 114). The width of this bridge suggests the flow of water along the River Fleete was much greater in times past. The terrace of six houses on the eastern side of the bridge is amongst the earliest in Teignmouth Road (Figure 110). The river then flowed through a copse which was eventually built on and became the modern houses of Winstone Avenue.

The route of the river now continues behind Winstone Avenue (Figure 115) and at its junction with Teignmouth Road (Figure 116) it disappears underground until it reaches Torquay Harbour and enters the sea. First it feeds the huge flood prevention tank at Hele Corner that is buried beneath Cuthbert Mayne School playing field.

Figure 111 - The little known thatched cottage in Coombe Lane
Figure 112 - the River Fleete flowing through the garden of the cottage

Figure 113 - The Fleete at the entrance to the playing field
Figure 114 – An old arched bridge in Combe Place

Figure 115 - The river flows behind Winstone Avenue
Figure 116 - The junction with Teignmouth Road

Figure 117 – Artist's impression of the construction of the flood prevention Tank beneath Cuthbert Mayne School playing field

The Fleete Valley is the natural route for excess water to reach the sea and historically there has been flooding along the course of the River Fleete at Hele Corner, Upton, Castle Circus, Union Street and Fleet Street (now renamed Fleet Walk). Flooding is not caused just by the volume of rainwater flowing in the River Fleete in periods of high rainfall. Flooding is also caused from the combined volume in the sewers, other watercourses, surface water runoff, highway drainage, groundwater and the sea during stormy spring tides.

The huge growth in population in Torquay in the 20th century has resulted in more homes, more concrete surfaces, more sewage and less green space leading to an increase in water flow and an increase in the risk of flooding. Compare Torquay in 2021 with the terrain in the 1869 OS map where much of the land was still covered with copses and meadows rather than buildings (Figure 121). Up to the end of the 18th century, the Fleete valley leading up from the harbour was a meadow and probably a flood plain. It is not surprising that the Fleete floods from time to time.

From Hele Corner the river flows under Teignmouth Road and through the Combe Valley limestone gorge between Daison Hill on its east bank and Windmill Hill and Stoney Combe on its west bank to reach Penney's Cottage (Figure 118). This superb 1870 photo was taken at a time when quarrying was still in progress. Before the commencement of the limestone quarrying the gorge was considerably narrower than it is in this photo, and in 2021 the gorge is now much wider on the west bank than that in the photo.

Figure 119 is a 2020 photo taken from the same spot with Penney's Cottage looking remarkably similar although road widening has reduced the size of the front gardens of Daison Cottages. The limestone wall bordering Daison quarry and Daison Woods shown in the photo still stands.

Figure 118 – The Fleete flowing through Combe Valley now Teignmouth Road
(Torquay Museum Archive PR4283 Teignmouth Road)

Figure 119 – Penney's Cottage and Daison Cottages 2020

Figure 120 – Pre 1870 cottages in the Combe Valley

    The Daison, a large house marked on the 1889 OS map (Figure 110), was built in 1850 but sold and demolished sometime after 1920 and Chatto, Dower and Westhill Roads and Main, First, Second and Third Avenues were built. The western border of the Daison estate was the River Fleete (Figure 110) and Daison Woods had many footpaths. Although much of the woods remain, the paths have long gone.

    At the edge of the woods in Teignmouth Road were Laurel Cottage and other buildings that were probably associated with the quarry. These have all gone. Both sides of the gorge now have modern industrial units. However, on its western side the four old cottages built before 1870 remain and are in excellent condition (Figure 120).

The River Fleete once flowed under at least four bridges in Upton: a bridge near Penney's Cottage at the bottom of Penny's Hill, one at the bottom of what is now Chatto Road, the old Upton Bridge at what is now the junction of Upton Road and Lymington Road, and the fourth was at the site of the Town Hall at Castle Circus. The site of the first three bridges can be identified from the 1869 OS map (Figure 121).

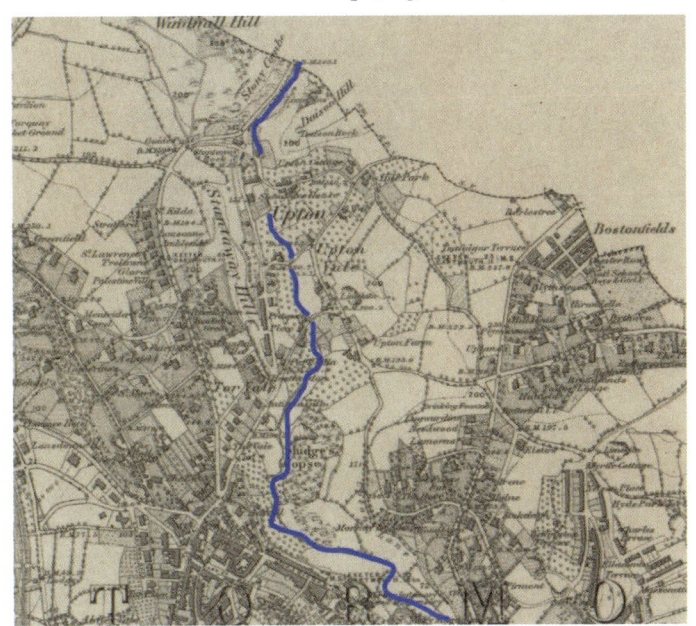

Figure 121 – The River Fleete from Combe Valley to the Castle Circus in 1869
(Reproduced with the permission of the National Library of Scotland)

In 1793 the Rev John Swete visited Torquay and painted a picture of the bridge at the bottom of Penny's Hill (Figure 122). He describes the stream as 'rapid' and the Combe Valley as having 'a range of mountainous craggy hills'. This confirms the suspicions that the River Fleete was considerably greater in size than a babbling brook. Penney's Cottage still exists albeit rebuilt after a fire in 2005. I've used the old spelling 'Penney's Cottage' for what is known today as 'Penny's Cottage'.

In 1897 and 1898 a major construction project was underway to pipe the River Fleete outside Daison Cottages which are opposite Penney's Cottage, and in Lymington Road near to the junction with Upton Road. The pipes were 36 inches in diameter and part of the town's flood prevention scheme.

The size of the old Upton Bridge in the scene from the second half of the 19th century (Figure 123) also indicates that the River Fleete had a significant flow of water. It stood at what is now the junction of Upton Road and Lymington Road. The bridge was a successor to the ancient Pitta Ford, suggesting that the lost name for the River Fleete was the Pitta. Serious flooding occurred here in the 1950s.

Figure 122 – The bridge at Penney's Cottage 1793 by Rev J Swete
(Reproduced by kind permission of Devon Archives & Local Studies, DHC 564M/F4)

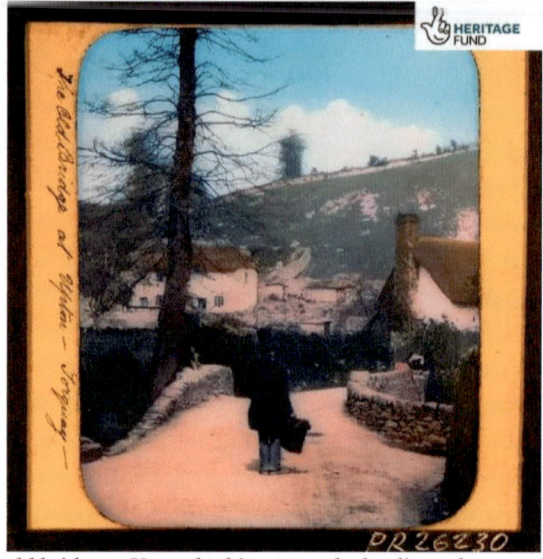

Figure 123 – The old bridge at Upton looking towards the disused quarry in St James Road
(Torquay Museum Archive PR26230)

The OS map published in 1869 (Figure 121) shows the route of the river Fleete from the site of old Upton Bridge through fields, copses and meadows to Castle Circus. In 2021 this translates into flowing under

Torquay Coach Station, Upton Park and behind the Torquay Town Hall. Buried under the section of Upton Park next to the coach station is another water attenuation tank built in the 1990s.

In 1869 the Victorian terraced-houses in Lymington Road had yet to be built, and what was to become Upton Park were still fields and copses. In the early 19th century 'Cockrem's Guide to Torquay' referred to Upton and suggests that: 'were houses built along the base of the hills, and the intervening space entirely laid out in pleasure grounds, Upton would, I believe, form one of the most favourable winter residences for invalids'. The terraces of Lymington Road of circa 1895 opposite Upton Park might not be quite the style of house the writer was alluding to or hoping for, but particularly in the summer when the trees are in leaf, Upton Park is a pleasant area of the town (Figure 124).

On the western side of Upton Park is Magdalene Road, behind which is yet another high cliff with its hidden and lost shafts of the iron mine of 1850. A little further downstream, also on the west bank is the old Torquay Infirmary opened in April 1853 (Figure 126) and replaced by Torbay Hospital in 1928. The old infirmary has been converted into apartments.

The River Fleete, still hidden, wends its way behind the Town Hall and under its lower ground floor level at what appears to be a seemingly impossible low elevation. However, roads, car parks and building levels have changed considerably over the last 150 years whereas the River Fleete although unseen is timeless despite being unromantically buried.

Figure 124 – Upton Park in the summer of 2020

Figure 125 – St Mary Magdalene spire high above the Town Hall
Figure 126 – The old Torquay Hospital

Figure 125 was taken from the lower ground service road of the Town Hall, itself built in 1913, and shows the spire of St Mary Magdalene Church consecrated on the 12 April 1849 high up on the top of a worked out quarry. It's another example of the gorge like route of the River Fleete.

The route of the river from Castle Circus to the harbour has an interesting history. Imagine Union Street and Fleet Walk being meadows, orchards and furze with just a few houses. Flowing down through today's town centre the River Fleete was joined by a brook cascading down from Ellacombe. It then entered a millpond which was on the site of the Union Hotel. But of course the Union Hotel no longer exists. The site of the millpond and the Union Hotel were more or less on the land opposite the Old Town Hall, which is at the junction of Abbey Road and Union Street.

The millpond fed the nearby and centuries-old Fleete Mill (Figure 127) which is mentioned in 17th-century deeds. The Rev John Swete describes the locality as one of quarries, trees and thickets. The waterwheel of the Fleete Mill kept turning until 1835 when the mill was demolished and the Union Hotel was built on the site of the millpond.

One of the millstones was used as a step in the porch of the Union Hotel and when it was demolished in the 1960s and replaced by shops, including, The International Stores, the millstone was given to Torquay Museum.

In 1807 the meadows of the Fleete Valley resembled the scene in Figure 128. It shows the road still known as Pimlico on the left-hand side and to its right is most likely the Fleete Mill. Then in 1826 the land was marked out in plots and the building commenced on both sides of what became Union Street and Fleet Street. The 'rabbit warrens' of Factory Row, Temperance Street and Lower Union Lane also came into existence. The individual shops, workshops and houses had little uniformity except that each had a front garden and iron railings. Fleet Street (now Fleet Walk) was built alongside the older George Street and Swan Street.

Figure 127 – The Fleete Mill 1793 by Rev John Swete
(Reproduced by kind permission of Devon Archives & Local Studies, DHC 564M/F4)

Figure 128 – The meadows of the Fleete Valley 1807 (Torquay Museum Society Library)

The River Fleete would have flowed from Castle Circus along the lowest parts of Union Street, Temperance St and Lower Union Lane where a few of the 19th-century buildings still stand. These streets were once a hive of activity of workshops, stores and homes. However, it does seem incredible that Torquay town centre still has buildings (Figures 130 and 131) in the 21st century that do not live up to its title of the English Riviera.

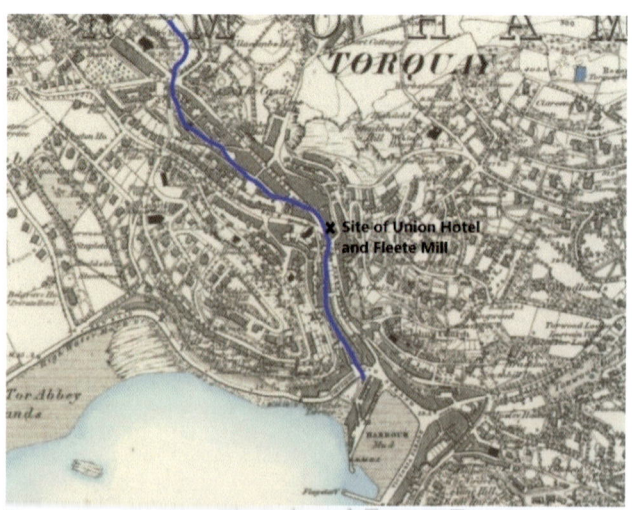

Figure 129 – The River Fleete through Torquay Town Centre 1869
(Reproduced with the permission of the National Library of Scotland)

Figure 130 – 19C building in Lower Union Lane Figure 131 – 19C workshop and home in Temperance Street

In the 19th century the River Fleete meadows were gradually transformed into a built up area and the river flowed along the cramped and narrow Swan Street and George Street to the harbour. Then in 1849 tragedy struck the inhabitants in Swan Street and George Street when 66 of the poorest died of cholera from the contaminated water of the River Fleete. It served as a source of drinking water and a sewer before emptying into the creek behind Vaughan Parade (Figure 135) before the major reclamation programme to create Cary Green.

It's ironic and tragic that two streets named after the wealthy Cary family of Torre Abbey should not only become the 19th-century slums of Torquay, but also hold this grim past. Swan Street was named after the Cary family emblem which was a swan and George Street after one of the many George Carys.

Figure 132 - The Fleete Valley in 1830 (Torquay Museum Society Library)

Figure 133 – The Fleete Valley in 1852 looking towards Torquay Harbour (Torquay Museum Society Library)

In 1864 proposals were made to widen Fleet Street. One suggestion was to sweep away most of George Street and in doing so would clean up the area of at least some of its slums. However, due to legal difficulties this did not happen and it took until 1989 for the two of the oldest streets in the town to be demolished when the Fleet Walk shopping centre was built (Figure 134).

To do so, a row of Victorian shops, similar to those further up on the left towards the roundabout, were demolished as were George Street and most of Swan Street. When the foundations for the new shopping centre were excavated the old culverts of the River Fleete were found. These have been preserved but covered over.

The concept of Fleet Walk was to have small speciality shops. KFC a fast food chicken-and-chips outlet wanted to locate there but planning permission at the time was refused. The idea of dozens of speciality shops did not happen and the shop units have never been fully occupied.

Figure 134 – Fleet Walk in 2018

For example, the 'Winter Garden' at the harbour end of Fleet Walk only ever had a handful of shops and was largely empty for many years. Then, Torbay Council had a change of policy. Wetherspoons and other pub chains now occupy the floor space of the Winter Garden. The large clothing and household chain of TK Maxx leased half of the first floor of Fleet Walk and KFC too moved into the complex.

In 1989 the town's buses were run by the Bayline Bus Company and used what were large minibuses and ideal in size for driving up and down Fleet Walk. The bus congestion and noise of the double-decker buses in use in 2021 came later.

The River Fleete has over the past 150 years burst its banks and lifted manhole covers and caused flooding in Union Street and Fleet Street. For example, the 'Torquay Directory' newspaper described the flooding that occurred on Friday 28 May 1875 in Union Street. A thunderstorm that lasted 'a little over a quarter of an hour caused considerable damage'. The rain fell in torrents and soon Union Street was 'filled by a rushing torrent which spread over the carriage road and footpaths alike, and being fed by streams that ran down from Ellacombe, soon flooded the lower part near the Town Hall' This area has flooded numurous times over the decades. The newspaper is referring to the old Town Hall at the junction of Abbey Road and Union Street (the building still exists). The newspaper article also informs 'that the water pressure was so great on the main sewer in Abbey Place that it burst up and flooded the shops close by'. Abbey Place was a town square at the very bottom of Fleet Street under which the main sewer flowed to empty into the sea near to where the pavilion stands.

A hundred years later in the 1970s there were numerous floods in the town centre, and between 1999 and 2012 there were five flooding incidents alone. The two massive water attenuation tanks at Upton and at Hele Corner along with improved drainage at the bottom of Union Street have reduced the risk of flooding, but with global warming and the increase in incidents of very heavy rain, time will tell how often the Fleete Valley floods again.

The tiny, unassuming stream at Watcombe grandly called the River Fleete has reached Torquay Harbour and although now in the 21st century it is largely hidden it has been an important feature for Torquay's inhabitants for centuries. Its journey and our journey from its source to the sea have indeed revealed much about the history of the town and its people.

Figure 135 – The creek behind Vaughan Parade in 1842 where the River Fleete met the sea (Torquay Museum Society Library)

Dedication

This study of the River Fleete is dedicated to my good friends who have helped to keep me sane during the 2020-2021 COVID-19 pandemic through their emails, telephone calls and encouragement: David Biggs, Sue Harwood, Alan and Joan Henshaw, Andrew Underhay and John Watt.

CHAPTER 6

A WALK AROUND TORQUAY HARBOUR

A walk around Torquay Harbour reveals so much about the history of the town over many hundreds of years, because the history of the harbour mirrors the history of the town and can be summed up in the word 'growth'.

Much of the history of Torquay is relatively recent. In 1800 it was still a small fishing village. Excluding St Marychurch, there were just 838 inhabitants living in the harbour area and up through what is now the town centre to Torre and Upton. By 1851 the population had already grown to 11,500. However, Torquay does have a maritime history that stretches back at least to the early part of the 16th century. A map, circa 1525, shows a pier at Torquay and maritime records reveal that in the reign of James 1 (1601-1625) there was a trading ship based at Torquay. Between 1625 and 1628 there was a Torquay ship used as a privateer – a privately owned armed ship authorised by the government for use in war especially in the capture of merchant ships. In other words it was a legal pirate ship. Later that century during the second Dutch War, Admiral Ruiter sent a landing party to Torquay in 1667, which 'burnt two small vessels lying in the little harbour of Torquay but did not injure the village'.

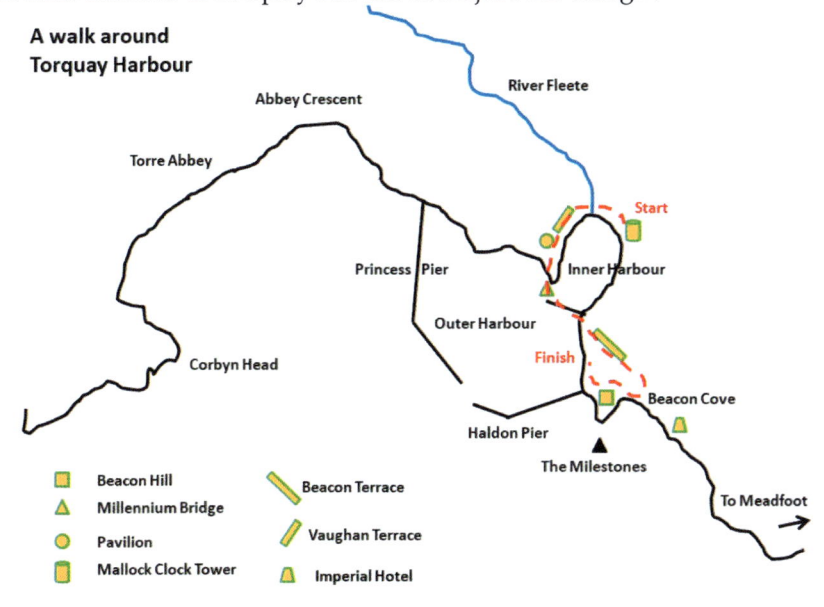

The route of our walk around the harbour starts at the Mallock Clock Tower on the Strand from where we will walk to Vaughan Parade, Cary Green, the Pavilion, North Pier, the Millennium Bridge, South Pier, Beacon Terrace, Beacon Cove, Haldon Pier and finishing at the D-Day slipways.

The Mallock Clock Tower (Figure 136) is a great place to start our walk and to study Torquay's harbour and its surroundings. Here, at the corner of Victoria Parade and the Strand, is where a pier stretched out diagonally into the sea to meet another constructed approximately 50 yards along Victoria Parade near to where the first quayside steps are.

Figure 136 – The Mallock Clock Tower on the Strand

Figure 137 – the harbour circa 1780 (Torquay Museum Archive PR26249)

The circa 1780 scene in Figure 137 shows both piers built of very large stones kept in place by very large logs or tree trunks sunk into the sea bed. The Rev John Swete's 1793 painting of the harbour also depicts two small piers. This first harbour was no more than one-eighth of the size of the

Inner Harbour but gave a measure of protection to the boats of local fisherman and to other vessels. There are only a dozen or so fishermen's houses in this old harbour area, and no buildings beyond the position of Beacon Quay by the Outer Harbour. There are no buildings at all on Beacon Hill which became the site of the old Marine Spa and the Living Coasts Zoo and there are none on Vane Hill, the bare hillside behind the harbour cottages. Torquay in 1780 is still a tiny village. But times are a-changing.

Situated behind where we are standing on the Strand was the London Inn (Figure 138). It commenced business in 1774 and was the first hotel and coach house in Torquay. Imagine the stage and post coaches leaving here each morning for Exeter and Dartmouth. By 1822 the hotel had a grand ballroom designed by John Foulston described by an Exeter newspaper as: 'the most splendid building of the sort of any watering place in the West of England'. In 1833 HRH Princess Victoria stayed at the hotel after which its name was changed to the Royal Hotel. School children formed two lines from the harbour steps where she disembarked to the hotel and she walked between these lines of children to it. From then on the harbour road name was changed to Victoria Parade.

Figure 138 – The Royal Hotel circa 1850 previously the London Inn
(Torquay Museum Library)

The archway at the far right-hand side of the hotel where the horse is being led still exists and is now the start of a footpath up to The Terrace. The Royal Hotel was extensive and stretched from the building behind the Clock Tower to the other side of the terracotta brick building in Figure 136.

Being Torquay's first hotel, the Royal Hotel was a catalyst for the early growth of the town and it was in the first 20 years of the 19th century that the population rapidly increased. There were two reasons for this.

During the Napoleonic Wars the English navy realised that Torbay was a safe anchorage. For example, in the spring of 1802, there were 30 warships in the bay in readiness for an attack from the French. What a sight that must have been.

The officers of the navy and their families wanted to stay in Torquay, and to meet their needs the Regency-style Higher Terrace high above the Strand (Figure 141) was built in 1811 as high class apartments and Lower Terrace was built around 1820 as fashionable lodging houses. From 1801 to 1821 the population of Torquay had doubled to 1,925.

Torquay was also 'built to accommodate invalids'. Its beneficial mild climate and sheltered bay was no doubt recommended by naval doctors to those who needed convalescence. One notable visitor was Elizabeth Barrett Browning who stayed at the Hotel Regina between 1838 and 1841 for health reasons.

Tradesmen and others also flocked to the town to find work and they lived in the terraces in Torre, Pimlico, George Street and Swan Street which were proudly named after George Cary of Torre Abbey and the Cary's family crest – the swan. Sadly, although George Street and Swan Street were very close to the harbour and surrounded by villas and mansions they would turn into overcrowded slums.

The Mallock Clock Tower was built in 1902 in memory of Richard Mallock of Cockington Court. He was the MP for Torquay for nine years between 1886 and 1895 and he faced up to being a large landowner on the edge of a rapidly expanding town. He was a man who 'served his neighbours well', so much so that the Clock Tower memorial to him was paid for by public subscription. It is constructed of yellow sandstone and sits on a limestone base and has some intricate carvings. It replaced a lamp standard that had been erected in 1887 to commemorate Queen Victoria's Golden Jubilee. Thankfully that was not destroyed and now stands in St Marychurch Precinct. The original white clock face of the tower was changed for a red clock face and illuminated with the gas lamps on each of the three corners, but again replaced in 1924 with another white clock face with an illuminated dial. The tower was restored in 2009.

In the early 19th century it was clear that the tiny harbour was too small to meet the needs of the growing town, when most of the building material and coal for the town and dried fish from Newfoundland was brought by ship to the harbour. In 1803 an Act of Parliament authorised the building of a new harbour which would be paid for by Sir Lawrence

Palk. His father was the Ashburton-born Robert Palk and a self-made man through his work with the East India Company resulting in his appointment as Governor of Madras. He became so wealthy that in 1768 he bought the Manor of Tormohun and became a major landowner in Torquay owning almost 1,500 acres of the town. The Palk family would have an important part to play in the development of the harbour area.

However, there was an intervention in the building of the new harbour by an extraordinary man. Dr Henry Beeke who was the son of a vicar of Kingsteignton rose to become the Dean of Bristol. He also had a reputation for 'fiscal authority' so much so that he assisted the government with the preparation of national budgets. Dr Beeke lived in Park Place in Torquay and was also a family friend and financial advisor to the Palk family. He questioned Sir Lawrence Palk's proposals for the new harbour because the original plans showed a very small north pier of about 50 yards long which was, in Dr Beeke's opinion, far too short to make a harbour suitable for ships to shelter in.

In the Palk family records held at the Devon Heritage Centre, a letter dated 1814 and written by Dr Beeke to Sir Lawrence Palk's solicitor, James Lambert, in London, explains that about five years earlier he had heard complaints from the inhabitants of Torquay that the new pier was totally useless and recommended that Sir Lawrence Palk should build a longer pier. Dr Beeke also suggests how to build a much less expensive pier. Although the harbour and its two piers under the original plan were completed in 1806 it does seem that they were extended soon after Dr Beeke's suggestion. On its completion North Pier separated the harbour from the shallow muddy creek where the River Fleete emptied into the sea and which subsequently would be filled in and become the site of Cary Green and the Pavilion.

We will now walk along the harbourside pavement on the Strand towards Vaughan Parade and stand at the slipway of the Inner Harbour. Surprisingly the photo of the Inner Harbour taken in September 2020 (Figure 139) and the 1832 print (Figure 140) have some remarkable similarities. These scenes that are separated by almost 200 years show a harbour slipway used then as now for launching small boats. Both have an avenue of trees to give shade when strolling along the path, when sitting and taking in the view, or when waiting for a bus or in 1832, for a donkey cart, horse and carriage, bath chair or sedan.

The 1832 view also shows the terrace of two-storied houses along Victoria Parade that were built in circa 1810. Just one of the houses remains making it one of the oldest buildings in Torquay and it is next door to the Queens Quay formally the Queen's Hotel. Whilst there is a seagull on the modern day slipway, I've yet to spot a seagull in the 1832 print.

The Queen's Hotel (Figure 139) was established in 1828 by Mr Joseph Marchetti on a site near Torquay's first baker's shop owned by Mrs Hutchings. However, despite the growth of the population of the town and the increase in the number of visitors Joseph Marchetti had difficulty in obtaining his licence. The vicar of Torre was opposed to it on the grounds that a second hotel would be prejudicial to the morals of the town and not surprisingly the landlord of the Royal Hotel was opposed too. Running a 'family hotel', Joseph Marchetti was no doubt undercutting the Royal Hotel on price.

The hotel has been rebuilt and restyled over the years. By 1892 it was called the Queen's Family Hotel and remodelled in 1937 into its familiar Art Deco style and named the Queen's Hotel. It underwent another refurbishment in 2009 and now in 2021 is divided into apartments and renamed yet again, this time to Queens Quay without the apostrophe even though there has never been a quay in the town by that name.

Figure 139 – Inner Harbour from Vaughan Parade in September 2020

The views of the harbour in Figure 135 from Vane Hill in circa 1842 and Figure 141 from South Pier in circa 1840 give a good feel of the growth of the harbour area. The old piers were swept away when the enlarged new harbour was built. Above the Strand is Higher Terrace built in 1811 and standing almost alongside it is the 1823 St John's Chapel. Vaughan

Terrace on Vaughan Parade was built in 1831. Behind Vaughan Terrace is a beach into where the River Fleete enters the sea and yet to be reclaimed to become Cary Green. In Figure 141 the Royal Hotel stands out as one of the largest buildings in the area.

Figure 140 – Inner Harbour circa 1832

Figure 141 – Torquay from South Pier circa 1840

Higher Terrace was built as nine fashionable residences and was one of Torquay's first early developments of Sir Lawrence Palk and erected in 1811. Its grandeur is enhanced by being a slightly bowed terrace with iron balconies, and there were canopy hoods over some of the windows. The principal rooms were on the first floor to take in the view of Tor Bay and not surprisingly the servants' quarters were in the basement. By 1851 the Torquay Natural History Society had its headquarters in Number 5 which was the centre house and the Society was trying to increase its membership with 'conversaziones, music, exhibits and bazaars'. The Society moved to its current museum building in Babbacombe Road in 1876.

St John's Chapel was built for the same reason as the harbour – to meet the needs of a growing town. In the first two decades of the 19th century there were only two places of worship in the town. There was the tiny Wesleyan Chapel in George Street and the parish church some way away in Torre so in 1818 it was decided to build a Chapel of Ease near to the harbour. It was completed in 1823. You might have noticed that the church in Figures 135 and 141 do not resemble the Grade I listed St John's Church that stands tall and overlooks the harbour in the 21st century. Its building commenced in 1863 and took 22 years to complete. It was well-worth the wait with its Devon marble, and its paintings, windows and mosaics by the finest 19th-century craftsmen from England and Italy.

The beach at the mouth of Torquay's River Fleete was gradually filled in with builders' rubble and spoil and the foundations for Vaughan Terrace were laid. This row of seven houses was built in 1831 by Sir Lawrence Vaughan Palk (son of Sir Lawrence Palk who had died in 1813) and named after his mother's maiden name. Like Higher Terrace it was built by Jacob Harvey. The terrace is double depth with front doors facing the Inner Harbour and others in Palk Street overlooking Cary Green. Over its life of nearly 200 years the terrace has understandably gone through a lot of renovation and additions.

Between Vaughan Terrace and the old Lloyds Bank of 1900 is a building of a different style but also built in 1831 by Jacob Harvey. It was at one time Cole's Library, billiard and public rooms. In 1846 it was altered to become the home of William Kitson, a solicitor, sometimes called 'The Maker of Torquay' in his role of head of the Palk Estates. He planned the layout of the roads in the Lincombes, Braddons and Warberries, and then parcelled off the land which were sold to wealthy incomers to build their villas on the slopes facing the sea. The house is now called Bank Chambers and for a considerable time were the offices of Kitson's solicitors before the company moved to its current location on the outskirts of Torquay at Edginswell. To the left of Vaughan Terrace is Carlton Chambers built in 1897. The ground floors of Bank Chambers, the old Lloyds Bank and Carlton Chambers are now in 2021 all restaurants and the upper floors are offices. We will now walk behind Vaughan Parade to Cary Parade, Palk Street and Cary Green.

In 2021, Cary Parade the road beyond Cary Green cannot be thought of as an attractive part of the town with its bus stops, taxi rank and ugly amusement arcades. But - just look behind those arcades for a glimpse of its former glory. It was in 1794 that a local architect by the name of Searle built a terrace of houses each with its small, neat front garden, known as New Quay and renamed Cary Parade. Two of those original houses are visible in Figure 143.

Figure 142 – Vaughan Parade in 2016

In Number 1 Cary Parade at the time of the 1841 and 1851 census lived the widow Amelia Griffiths (1768-1858), her two daughters, cook, housemaid and footman. Amelia had moved to Torquay in 1829 and was already an acknowledged seaweed expert and was dubbed the Queen of Algologists (the branch of botany that studies seaweed and algae). She combed the beaches of Torquay for seaweeds with her great companion Mary Wyatt who kept a pressed plant shop in Torquay. The seaweeds were preserved and the collections are in Torquay Museum and the Royal Albert Memorial Museum in Exeter.

The Torbay Hotel was also an early hotel in the town and its history dates back to 1854 whilst Delmonte, formally Rock House was one of Torquay's early villas and built circa 1840. It is now divided into apartments and vehicular access is via Rock Road.

Cary Green in 2021 has plenty of interesting features. There is a sculpture by Carole Vincent just visible in the right hand side of Figure 143 celebrating the 1988-1989 Year of the Pedestrian. There is a sundial (a gift from the McDonald's fast foods company) opposite the Pavilion commemorating the centenary in 1992 of the Incorporation of Torquay as a Borough. Then there is another sculpture which is of Agatha Christie. It was unveiled on 10 September 1990 to commemorate the centenary of her birth in Torquay on 15 September 1890.

Figure 143 – Cary Green looking towards Cary Parade

Figure 144 – Torquay Pavilion

On the seaward side of Cary Green is the once magnificent Torquay Pavilion and, if there is a building in Torquay that is dear to the hearts of Torquinians, it is that building. Torquay Council had since its 1892 incorporation as a borough wanted to provide high class visitor attractions in both summer and winter. There were many proposals for a pavilion in the harbour area and the site chosen was the tennis courts next to the coal stores in Princess Gardens shown in Figure 145.

The Pavilion was opened on 12th August 1912 and the newspapers of the land proclaimed it as 'The White Palace'. Built as a ballroom and assembly hall it rests on a floating raft of concrete and steel on reclaimed land. It is a fantasy design, with green copper domes, green tiles, fine Art Nouveau ironwork and four octagonal summer houses where afternoon tea was served. It had an oak-panelled cafe. However, the life of the Pavilion has passed through several phases. There was its illustrious phase. For a quarter of a century the Pavilion was the home of the municipal orchestra when Sir John Barbirolli and Sir Edward Elgar amongst others conducted it. In 1930 it was converted to a conventional theatre and, as a boy in the 1950s and 1960s, I remember it, with its red velvet seats.

Figure 145 – Princess Gardens in 1903

The Pavilion then entered its neglect phase when its upkeep was indeed neglected and in 1973 it was almost demolished but thankfully it had a reprieve. Then in 1977 it closed after years of summer shows including performances by the popular comedians Eric Sykes and Harry Worth.

The popular tourist attraction phase commenced and the Pavilion was restored and converted into an indoor artificial ice rink and leisure centre. I skated there once or twice reliving my boyhood roller skating days. But the ice rink did not last either and around the time that the Fleet Walk shopping development opened in 1989 the Pavilion too became another speciality shopping arcade. By 2013 it needed millions spent on it for repair and refurbishment and it moved into its closure phase that year pending development. One proposal was that it would become the entrance to an eleven floor hotel and apartment block but this was refused on environmental and other grounds. In 2021 Torquay waits to find out if the Pavilion can enter another phase of its life.

The site of the coal stores is now a two-storey car park and continues to do little to enhance the area except by providing a high walkway facing the Inner Harbour with green octagonal shelters mimicking those of the

Pavilion. Walking from the Pavilion we reach North Pier which has been in the 19th, 20th and 21st centuries a working pier for fishermen. It is a reminder that Torquay was once a fishing village and its tradition remains to this day.

Figure 146 – North Pier on the left and the 21st-century Millennium Bridge

Between the two World Wars a daily fish market was held at the pier where my grandfather, Edwin Lipscombe, who was a fish seller, bought his fish early each workday morning. His was a hard life. He lived in Barton Hill Road and pushed his fish trolley more than two miles from his home to North Pier to make his purchase and then pushed the trolley around the town selling the fish, before walking home. The right-hand image of Figure 147 is outside Torquay Museum in Babbacombe Road where his scales and at least five species of fish are in the trolley compartments.

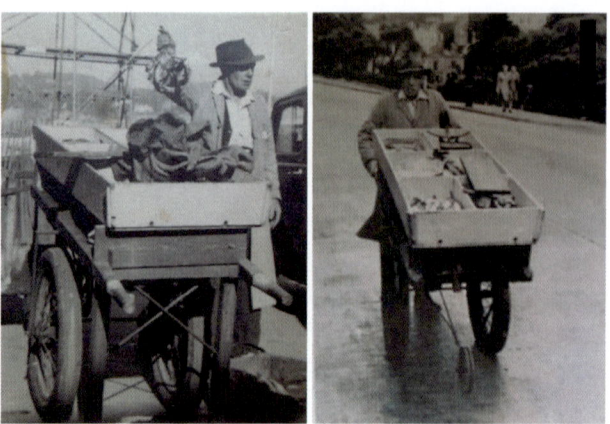

Figure 147 – Edwin Lipscombe, fish seller at North Pier and Babbacombe Road

If you were familiar with the harbour prior to 2003, you will be aware that the Inner Harbour was tidal and was often dirty and smelly at low tide when the beach was exposed. Even back in 1840 the stench was so bad from seaweed and the flotsam and jetsam brought in by the tide that a horse and cart had to take away the offending items.

It was not until 2003 that this situation improved when Torquay's waterfront had a £21 million redevelopment and taking centre stage was the new state-of-the-art Millennium Bridge linking North Pier and South Pier (Figure 146). The bridge includes a mid tide sill that traps the sea in the Inner Harbour at times of low tide. The sometimes noxious and sludgy harbour bed is now no longer visible, and the Inner Harbour is far more picturesque because water is kept at or above the mid-tide depth. The other novelty is that the pedestrian walkway is lifted to allow boats to pass in and out of the Inner Harbour during high tide. Torquay has its own miniature version of Tower Bridge. The linking of the two piers is also a great tourist attraction in itself and an asset to the town.

Having walked over the Millennium Bridge from North Pier we are at the pier head of South Pier, where in the second half of the 19th century, it had an unusual feature (Figure 148). It was a Barking Furnace. There are six narrowing steps that lead to a platform and inside this platform was a furnace with a copper pot on top of it. This pot contained beech and fir tree bark and water, which were boiled into creosote. This was then used by fishermen to treat their nets as a preservative. The cotton or hemp nets were dipped into the pot and then hung out to dry. The name 'Barking' is derived from the fact that the creosote was made from tree bark.

The furnace was still in use in the early 1900s but how long fishermen had been preserving their nets on the harbourside is unclear. The furnace was given to the fishermen by Lady Erskine who lived in Torquay sometime after 1853 and up to circa 1882 when Lord Erskine died. The furnace was closed to use by the fishermen around the time of World War II and the hole in the platform in which the copper bowl was placed has been cemented over, and a fixed harbour light has been installed on it.

From the South Pier it is a short walk to the Hotel Regina on the corner of Vaughan Parade, Beacon Hill and Beacon Quay (Figure 149). It was built around 1817 as a two-storey building and originally called The Bath House in which the first baths in Torquay were built for Dr Pollard. An 1817 guide book informs us that the baths offered 'hot, tepid, vapour, shower and cold sea water baths'. Torquay was indeed 'built to accommodate invalids', but also for those who visited the town for these invigorating health improving treatments.

Figure 148 – The Barking Furnace on South Pier

Another claim to fame for the Hotel Regina is that it was where the poet Elizabeth Barrett Browning stayed between 1838 and 1841 for health reasons. When she was aged just fifteen she became ill and suffered from intense head and spinal pain for the rest of her life, rendering her frail. She lived in Apartment 1 which was over the shop to the left of the archway (Figure 150), and then in Apartment 3, where the hotel's lounge is now situated by the hotel's main entrance. When she returned to London in September 1841, it is said that the inside of her carriage had a bed upon 'a thousand springs'.

Figure 149 – The Bath House and Beacon Terrace circa 1833 (St John's Church Archive)

Figure 150 – Hotel Regina 2020

The hotel baths became redundant in 1853 when the Medical Baths opened on Beacon Quay but the hotel continues to trade and now, 200 years later, the Hotel Regina is Torquay's oldest hotel. In 1929 when lifts were being installed the builders found some old baths under the drawing room. I enquired about these in 2018, but they have long gone and were no doubt broken up by the workmen. However, I discovered that other artefacts had been found in 2008 under the floorboards during renovations. Throughout World War II the hotel was used as accommodation by the RAF Air Sea Rescue Flotilla personnel, who were stationed at Haldon Pier. The builders found a hoard of World War II newspapers, mugs albeit broken embossed with the RAF badge, a Morse Code exercise sheet, a Penguin book entitled 'Aircraft Recognition', and even RAF laundry tickets issued by Torquay Laundries in Hele Road.

Our walk continues up Beacon Hill with time to admire Beacon Terrace. The houses must have looked brand spanking new to Elizabeth Barrett Browning because they were built in 1833, just 5 years before she stayed at the Hotel Regina. The terrace was built by Jacob Harvey, who was responsible for the finest early 19th-century houses in Torquay and we have already mentioned Higher Terrace and Vaughan Terrace. Other fine terraces included Lisburne Crescent in Higher Woodfield Road built in 1851 and Hesketh Crescent above Meadfoot Beach built in 1848. The ten houses of Beacon Terrace have alternate external features. All have cast iron balconies but with the odd numbers having one long balcony shade whilst the even numbers have small sunshades over each of their three first floor windows, separated by attractive columns (except Number 8 which is a larger house and has another design). The balcony shades on Numbers 6 and 7 have been removed.

Behind Beacon Terrace is an extremely high retaining wall and between the terrace and this wall are the almost sunless workers cottages. The high wall and cottages can be seen from around the corner in Park Hill Road. In 1858, disaster struck. The retaining wall gave way and fell into the back of Numbers 2, 3 and 4, tragically killing the Hambling family in Number 4, whilst the Tanners and Helliers were dug out of Numbers 2 and 3.

The 1843 building next to Beacon Terrace is a completely different design and is the home of the Royal Torbay Yacht Club which was formed in 1863. Sailing had been popular since 1813 when Torquay introduced its annual regatta called the 'Torbay Royal Regatta'.

On 8 May 1942, His Majesty King George VI visited Torquay and from the public sitting area just above the Royal Torbay Yacht Club, he reviewed units of the Royal Air Force stationed in Torquay for training during World War II.

Across the road from the Yacht Club there is a path down to Beacon Cove which is where we will now visit. However, we will pause at the entrance to the beach path where, on an adjacent wall, is a plaque remembering a sad and tragic event. It reads:

> 'To remember John Moran of St Vincent's Home for Boys who died in the Marine Spa Swimming Pool at this site on 13 July 1971 aged 11 years. Remembered with affection by all who knew him especially by his friends from St Vincent's. This plaque was provided by Torbay Council on behalf of the people of Torquay.'

On 13 July 1971 three children including eleven-year-old John Moran from St Vincent's Children's Home in Torre were enjoying their swimming lessons in the Marine Spa swimming pool that was on this very spot where we now are standing. But somehow, and there has never been a satisfactory answer, John was sucked down the ten-inch outlet pipe and drowned. Despite the efforts of workman with pneumatic drills who worked throughout the night, John could not be saved. Even now, 50 years later, I feel as a Torquinian immensely sad about this tragedy which surely should never have been allowed to happen. I had swum there many times in the 1960s when I was schoolboy and the thought that this accident could have happened to me, my twin sister or my friends is frightening. By September that year the Marine Spa and its swimming pool were demolished.

Beacon Cove is the nearest beach to the harbour (ignoring the Inner Harbour at low tide before the construction of the Millennium Bridge) and even in 1817 a guidebook states: 'a small cove near the town affords a fine beach for bathers'. At some point in the 19th century and until 1900, men and women were segregated when it came to swimming. Beacon Cove became a ladies bathing beach and men had to swim at Peaked Tor Cove which is situated on the other side of the Imperial Hotel.

In the 20th century Beacon Cove became incredibly popular as is evident in the pre-World War II photo (Figure 151). Most beach goers are sitting in deck chairs with sensible sunshades and 'floats' could be hired which were an early version of 21st-century sea kayaks and paddleboards.

Changing tents maintained modesty and refreshments were served at the redundant lifeboat house. Torquay's first lifeboat, 'The Mary Brundret' was launched on 22 May 1876 and the third and last lifeboat in Torquay, 'The Wighton', ceased service in 1923.

During the 1960s Beacon Cove was still very popular and there was a diving board fixed to the cliff on the far side of the beach. However, in the 1970s its popularity declined and its story is entwined with the story of Beacon Hill, the Marine Spa and Living Coasts Zoo.

Figure 151 – Beacon Cove circa 1930

In 2021, Beacon Cove is not even a shadow of its former self. All that remains are the beach promenade and steps (Figure 152). There is no cafe, diving board or deckchairs for hire. It is an uninviting place that has attracted trouble, so much so, that there is a security gate at the beginning of the beach path that is locked overnight to prevent access.

To the right of Beacon Cove is Beacon Hill that was the site of the Living Coasts Zoo and part of the Wild Planet Trust that cares for Paignton and Newquay Zoos. It opened in 2003 and the outdoor section was covered in the huge netted tent to prevent the sea birds escaping and flying away. There were penguins and seals outside which could also be seen diving in their pools from inside Living Coasts. Also inside was an aquarium with puffer fish and a sting ray, plus plenty of children's activities including a tunnel to climb through above which was an aquarium tank. Another attraction was a scary animatronic Great White Shark. One aspect of the Living Coasts cafe that was particularly enjoyable was its sun terrace that overlooked Beacon Cove and was usually a sheltered spot to enjoy the view and a coffee. Unfortunately Living Coasts like many visitor attractions was closed during the 2020 COVID-19 pandemic lockdown. The resultant drop in income caused it to become less than viable and it closed permanently in the summer of 2020. The sea birds, penguins, seals and other marine creatures have been rehoused in other zoos.

Figure 152 – Beacon Cove 2020

Rewinding back to the first half of the 19th century, Beacon Hill was a large promontory of limestone rock that would have filled the space inside the Living Coasts netted tent. By 1852 the growing town of residents and visitors required bathing facilities greater than Dr Pollard could provide at the Bath House. The face of Beacon Hill on the harbour side was partially cut away to provide space for the new Bath Saloons built behind Shaw's Shipbuilding Yard, that is just about visible in Figure 153 and it opened in September 1853. An article on the 1860 'Torquay Directory' newspaper records that the Bath Saloons offered a range of bath treatments similar to that offered by Dr Pollard at the Bath House: cold and tepid, fresh or sea water plunge, vapour and douche.

The Bath Saloons also included a large reading room where before and after treatments patrons could relax. Charles Dickens visited in 1862 and gave two-hour daily readings. In 1855 improvements were made to Beacon Cove with the building of a breakwater as a defence against rough seas. However, after just four years it was destroyed in the storm of 1859. A seawater swimming pool was opened in 1857 and it had four rugged open arches (Figure 154) with access to the sea at all times. The Bath Saloons and its facilities became a huge asset to the town but was not a financial success.

Torquay continued to grow and there was an urgent need to provide a safe anchorage for larger vessels, and a facility where ships could berth at all tides and not dependent on a high tide to enter the Inner Harbour.

In 1861 Sir Lawrence Palk proposed to build and pay for a much larger and complex harbour. The plan was to construct a 700 foot breakwater (approximately half the length of Brixham Breakwater) from the other side of the Imperial Hotel at Lands End heading west in the direction of Livermead Beach then turning towards the Inner Harbour to meet a new 200 foot pier extending from North Pier in a south westerly direction also heading towards Livermead, then turning 90 degrees in a south easterly direction for another 250 feet. The plan was approved but never started, but just imagine the size this harbour would have been and how it would have changed the face of Beacon Cove and the current harbour area.

A second plan was put into place – the building of Haldon Pier. The remainder of Beacon Hill was quarried and flattened and the stone used to make 20-ton blocks of rock. For every 20 feet of pier, 75 of these blocks were needed. Haldon Pier was opened in August 1870 by Sir Lawrence Palk – Lord Haldon.

The flattening of Beacon Hill provided the opportunity to develop the Bath Saloons and build the main hall that over the decades was used as a palm court when the room was filled with palm trees and other exotic plants, a skating rink, a badminton hall and a ballroom. The original ballroom in the 1853 building became a lounge. In 1916 the old 1857 swimming pool was replaced with a 90-feet-by-30-feet indoor sea water pool alongside the main hall and to do so more excavation of Beacon Hill was required. The pool had three arched windows facing onto Beacon

Cove and a large roof window. As a boy I had many good times at the swimming pool with its changing rooms all along each side of the pool, with what seemed at the time very high diving boards. However it is in this pool that John Moran drowned.

Figure 153 – Torquay Harbour circa 1850

Figure 154 – The arches of the 1857 swimming pool that were open to the sea

By 1922 the Bath Saloons was one of the leading spas in the country and to maintain its reputation, the largest sun lounge in the country was opened in 1929. Called the Vita glass sun lounge it was 90 feet by 18 feet and overlooked Beacon Cove. The Bath Saloons also had a south facing 'cooling lounge' where those who had completed their treatments could relax. No doubt this rest was needed to get over any electric shock treatment or a seaweed bath.

Around 1931 the name of the complex was updated to 'Torquay Marine Spa' and it kept this name until its demise and demolition in 1971 following that tragic death of John Moran. There were protests about its demolition but, after that awful drowning, the pool certainly could not reopen and with the desire to move with the times the fate of the old Bath Saloons and its ballroom was sealed. The Beacon Hill site awaited its redevelopment.

Six years later in 1977 the site had been redeveloped into the Coral Island entertainment centre. It was an ugly jungle of concrete, and a 'White Elephant' from the word go (Figure 155). Despite efforts to attract customers with its outdoor pool and sun terraces, a disco, slot machines, wrestling, bingo, bars and restaurants, the complex closed in September 1988. For more than a decade the derelict building site was an embarrassment being on Torquay's prime site overlooking the harbour, Beacon Cove and Tor Bay. It was eventually demolished in 1997. It took another six years before Paignton Zoo took the initiative to create Living Coasts which opened in 2003, but as mentioned, during the COVID-19 pandemic lockdown of 2020, it closed. Its huge drop in income forced it to follow in the footsteps of the Marine Spa and Coral Island. The site once more awaits its new lease of life.

Figure 155 – Coral Island circa 1980 (Torquay Museum Archive PR16960)

We will now walk up the path from Beacon Cove and along the top level of the Beacon Quay multi-storey car park to stand at its railings overlooking the Outer Harbour. The panorama is superb with a tremendous view of the harbour and the surrounding area. On our left is the huge netted-tent of Living Coasts through which and behind which are glimpses of the Imperial Hotel. Also on our left is the footbridge to the Living Coasts terrace with its glorious views across the bay.

Haldon pier stretches out in front of us and together with Princess Pier form the Outer Harbour. Below us on Beacon Quay and adjoining Haldon Pier is the recently-built public slipway for the launching of private craft and next to it is the landing stage for the ferry services to Brixham and Paignton. To its right are the two D-Day landing slipways. Along the length of the quay is the unique D-Day 'Vanishing Point' memorial. The Outer Harbour is also the home of Torquay Marina where hundreds of boats of all sizes moor alongside the marina jetties.

Beyond the Outer Harbour and in the distance are Corbyn Head, the Grand Hotel, and Torre Abbey Sands behind which and hidden by trees is the ancient Torre Abbey. Also behind the beach is the Belgrave Hotel and the 2015 Abbey Sands Development renamed Abbey Crescent. Above Rock Walk is Waldon Hill with its apartment blocks overlooking the harbour and, at the base of Rock Walk, is the Princess Theatre.

Further to our right is South Pier on which a large red crane stands waiting to lift boats in and out of the harbour. Behind it are glimpses of the Millennium Bridge, the Pavilion, Vaughan Terrace and St John's Church. Behind us is the Hotel Regina and Beacon Terrace above which on the sky line is the Italianate Villa Lugano. Surely this 360-degree vista has to be the best view from any multi-storey car park in the country.

But the scene described would not be complete without the tourists and residents enjoying a day out sitting outside the cafes and walking along Haldon Pier. Nor would it be complete without the yachtsmen attending to their boats and the ferries sailing to and from Brixham and Paignton.

Beacon Quay has had over the last 200 years a varied history. There was a shipyard on the quay maybe for centuries and it was closed in 1870 when Haldon Pier was built. Electricity came to Torquay in 1898 when an electricity generating station was opened on Beacon Quay. The site was chosen because of the ease of bringing in coal and the obvious supply of water to power the generator. The station was expanded in 1902 and again in 1911, 1913 and 1914 and not surprisingly there were complaints from those living in the harbour area about the volume of smoke emitted from the generators. One solution was to build a generator in the Upton Valley but nothing came of this. The town had to wait until after World War I when in 1924 the town's electricity supply was provided from the large power station next to Newton Abbot Railway station.

In the 1930s cars parked on Beacon Quay facing the Outer Harbour but it was still very much a working quay. Coal was still shipped from the collieries of the north of England and stored in coal stores at Beacon Quay. The harbourmaster's office was in a single-storied building.

With the onset of World War II Torquay, like many seaside towns, would play its part in the defence of our country. Two embarkation slipways were built in 1943 in readiness for an invasion of France. On the 5 June 1944 the US 4th Infantry Division embarked from these slipways and the troops landed at Utah Beach in Normandy at 6.30 am on 6 June 1944.

After the war Torbay was chosen as the venue for the yacht races for the 1948 Olympic Games no doubt because the D-Day slipways gave good access for the boats taking part.

From thence onwards the same slipways were used by locals and tourists to launch their own boats. The slipways were a great place to fish from and as a boy in the 1960s, I enjoyed many sunny days by dropping a line down through the slots in the slipways trying to catch tiny wrasse and the eight inch long smelt.

By the 1990s the slipways were showing their age and becoming unsafe, and Torbay Council wanted to demolish them. Thankfully, due to the strength of feeling by the people of Torquay of the historic importance of the slipways, they had a reprieve and were given Grade II listed status in 2000. Historic England describes them as 'extremely rare survivals, these slipways are possibly the best-surviving example of D-Day fabric in the country'. Now fenced off by railings for obvious safety reasons they are part of the town's memorial to the troops using them back in 1944 and have become a tourist attraction in their own right.

By the late 1950s the quay was changing from a working quay to a leisure quay and the old buildings on the quay were swept away. By 1961 the three-level multi-storey car park had been built. It is said that on its opening day of the 23 June 1961 the top level became full within an hour. It continues to be a busy and well used car park.

The ground floor level of the building was used as a boat salesroom, chandlers and for the town's marine aquarium, 'Aqualand'. It included local sea life and, perhaps strangely, a large turtle that lived in a tank that was far too small for it. On my visits to Aqualand as a boy, and when I was older with my son, I always thought it was cruel to keep such a creature in those conditions. The aquarium was always dark, dimly lit and damp but none the less interesting. A 19th-century Torquay connection with Aqualand is that the inventor of the marine aquarium was marine biologist Philip Gosse who lived at Sandhurst in St Marychurch Road where he is remembered there with a Torbay Civic Society Blue Plaque. Aqualand closed in the mid 1980s.

Figure 156 – the two D-Day slipways and the Vanishing Point memorial

We will end our walk around Torquay Harbour at the departure point of the US troops in 1944 which is now remembered by an unusual work of art by Bob Budd called 'The Vanishing Point' (Figure 156). Standing at an illuminated cross set into the ground at the entrance to Beacon Quay, the eye is led towards the large ring representing a mooring ring. Then, set into the long wooden decking on the quay, is a row of lights spelling 'Vanishing Point' in Morse Code. Following this row of lights through the ring allows one to imagine the embarkation of the US 4th Infantry Division as they set out in large numbers of landing craft on 5 June 1944 to slowly vanish across the sea. This memorial was officially opened on 6 June 2015 when I had the privilege to be present as well as some local dignitaries. More importantly the ceremony was attended by some US veterans of the 4th Infantry Division. It was a very moving occasion.

Our walk around Torquay Harbour is at an end. It has revealed that it has been used for many centuries by fishermen, privateers, merchants, tourists, yachtsmen and the military. In the past 200 years the harbour has grown and changed to match the growing and changing needs of the population of both residents and visitors. It is inevitable that other changes will occur. For example, the Beacon Hill site requires a new use to replace Living Coasts and the Pavilion desperately needs a new life and identity. However, there is still much to see and enjoy.

Dedication

This chapter is dedicated to my grandson Leo Trewin who provided information and memories about Living Coasts.

REFERENCES

Aggett T (1888) The Demon Hunter - a legend of Daddy's Hole Plain, Torquay
Anon (1850) Legends of Torquay
Biography of Sir James Morrison online at https://www.jjhc.info/morrisonjameswilliam1856
Bainbridge (2005) Torquay a history and celebration
Bridges M (1842) Babbicombe or Visions of Memory with other Poems
Edmonds F S (1925) Chronicles of St Mary Church
Ellis A C (1930) An Historical Survey of Torquay
Fraser I (2008) The Palk Family of Haldon House and Torquay
Hinchliffe D (2020) The Drinking Fountains of Torquay
https://historicengland.org.uk/
https://maps.nls.uk/
https://osborneapartments.co.uk/2018/10/25/a-brief-history-of-hesketh-crescent/
htpps://www.ancestrylibraryedition.co.uk
https://www.torbay.gov.uk
Giddy & Giddy (1905) Sale brochure for Rock End, Torquay: Held at Torquay Museum Society Library
Gosse E (1907) Father and Son
Gosse P (1853) A Naturalist's Rambles on the Devonshire coast
Gosse P (1860) A History of the British Sea Anemones and Corals
Gosse P (1865) A Year on the Shore
Herald Express (1998) South Devon Bygones Supplement
Morrison J (1851) Diary of Sir James Morrison - held at Torquay Museum Library
Meadfoot Beach Chalets online at: https://www.dailymail.co.uk/news/article-3243966/
Oppenheim M (1968) The Maritime History of Devon
Pateman L L MBE compiler (1991) Pictorial & Historical Survey of Babbacombe & St Marychurch Volume II
Pearce F (2000) The Torquay Marine Spa
Pearce F (2002) Torbay the Golden Years
Perkins J W (1971) Geology Explained in South and East Devon
Pike J (1973) Torquay, Torbay: a bibliographical guide
Pike J R (1994) Torbay Heritage - Torquay
Pike J R (2001) Torquay a photographic history of your town

Read B (2015) Cockington Bygones
Russell P (1960) A History of Torquay
Seymour D J (1977) Torre Abbey
Seymour D J (1963) Upton - The Heart of Torquay
The Illustrated London News, 14 August 1852
Torquay and Tor Directory Newspapers - held at Torquay Museum Library
Torbay Council (2005) Barton Conservation Area Character Appraisal
Torbay Council (2005) Maidencombe Conservation Area Character Appraisal
Torbay Council (2005) St Marychurch Conservation Area Character Appraisal
Torbay Libraries (c2010) The Torbay Olympic Regatta
Trewman's Flying Post, 25 August 1853.
Tudor G (2007) Brunel's Hidden Kingdom
The System film archive at https://www.reelstreets.com/films/system-the/
Walker C (c1904) The Churches and Chapels of Torquay
Walker H H (1968) The Causeway near Torre Abbey in South Devon
Walker H H (1969) Torquay Museum Society - the first 125 years
White's Devonshire Directory of 1850
Wickes M (1985) Editor of John Wesley in Devon 1739 – 1789 extracts from his journals

INDEX

Abbey Crescent, 7, 10, 22, 23, 25, 26, 27, 28, 29, 30, 31, 34, 35, 37, 39, 40, 41, 42, 43, 142
Abbey Gates, 8, 14
Abbey Place, 119
Aggett, Joseph, 81
Aggett, Thomas, 56, 58, 62
Anstey's Cove, 66, 98, 99, 100, 101, 102
Aqualand, 143
Artillery Volunteers, 11
Avenue Road, 8
Babbacombe, 3, 19, 30, 55, 64, 67, 68, 70, 71, 87, 96, 97, 101, 102
Babbacombe Downs, 66, 67, 68, 70, 92, 96, 98
Badcock, John, 4
Badcott, George, 70
Badcott, John, 68
Badcott, Mark, 72, 99, 101
Badcott, Raymond, 64, 99, 101
Badcott, Sam, 68
Badcott, Trevor, 21
Ball, Susan, 71
Barbirolli, Sir John, 131
Barking Furnace, 133, 134
Barrett Browning, Elizabeth, 124, 134, 135
Barton, 11, 67, 73, 77, 78, 79, 81, 85, 86, 87, 101, 103, 104
Barton Quarry, 77, 79, 84, 104
Bayline Bus Company, 119
Beacon Cove, 62, 122, 136, 137, 138, 140, 141
Beacon Hill, 123, 133, 135, 138, 139, 140, 141

Beacon Quay, 123, 133, 135, 141, 142, 144
Beacon Terrace, 122, 134, 135, 136, 142
Beeke, Dr Henry, 125
Belgrave Hotel, 26, 28, 142
Belgrave Road, 3, 8, 10, 26, 34, 50
Bishop Phillpotts, 72
Bishopstowe, 72
Bowden, William, 81
Bridges, Matthew, 66, 67, 87, 88, 89, 90, 101
Brunel, Isambard Kingdom, 75, 84
Captain Peppers, 41
Cary Green, 117, 122, 125, 127, 128, 129, 130
Cary Parade, 128, 129
Cary, R S S, 10, 26, 28, 38
Cary, Sir George, 9
Cary, Sir Lucius, 8
Castle Circus, 105, 108, 111, 112, 114, 115
Chelston, 1, 3, 14, 15
Chestnut Avenue, 8
Christie, Agatha, 2, 129
Chudleigh, 4
Church Road, 79, 84
Clennon Lane, 79
Coastguard, 62, 63, 64, 65, 70,
Cockington, 1, 3, 9, 12, 13, 14, 15, 23, 124
Colonnade, 31, 34, 36, 38, 41
Compton Castle, 9
Coombe Lane, 105, 106, 107
Coral Island, 141
Corbyn Beach, 14, 22, 32

Corbyn Head, 11, 12, 26, 50, 142
Court Cottage, 13
Court House, 13, 87, 88
Cresswell, Brian and Carole, 82
Cross, John, 13
Cumper's Hotel, 6
Daddy's Hole, 20, 53, 58
Daddyhole Cove, 55, 56
Daddyhole Plain, 44, 48, 52, 53, 54, 55, 56, 57, 59, 61, 62, 63, 65
Daison Cottages, 109, 110, 111
Daison Hill, 16, 109
Dance, George, 25
Daw, Miss, 85, 86
Daw, Mr, 80
D-Day 'Vanishing Point' memorial, 142
D-Day slipways, 122, 142, 143
Delmonte, 129
Devil's Hole, 20, 44, 53, 56, 61, 62
Devon Marble, 2, 128
Dickens, Charles, 139
Doney, Suzannah 13
Drake, Sir Francis, 6, 9
Drinking fountain, 52
Ducking Stool, 12, 13
Dyer, John, 29
Edwards, Evan, 80, 81
Elgar, Sir Edward, 131
Ellacombe, 114, 119
Ellicombe, Jagnetta, 29
Ellicombe, Lucy, 29
Ellis, Robert, 81
Elm Avenue, 8
Erskine, Lady, 133
Falkland Road, 8
Fleet Walk, 16, 105, 108, 114, 115, 118, 119, 131
Fleete Mill, 114

Flower's Watermill, 13, 15
Frobisher, Sir Martin, 6
Gallows Gate, 12
Gasking, Mr, 70
George Street, 26, 115, 116, 117, 118, 124, 128
Gifford, Jon, 65
Gilbert, Sir John, 9
Goats' Path, 17, 90
Gosse Chapel, 73
Gosse, Edmund, 18, 66, 67, 68, 73, 75, 77, 79, 80, 84, 96, 98, 100
Great Hill, 66, 86, 87, 103
Greenway, 9
Griffiths, Amelia, 129
Haldon Pier, 62, 122, 135, 139, 141, 142
Hall, John, 81
Hall, William 81
Hambling family, 136
Hampton House, 69, 72, 96
Happaway Road, 77, 81, 105, 106
Harvey, Emma, 25
Harvey, John, 23
Harvey, J T and W, 20, 45
Hawkins, John 6
Hellier family, 136
Henley, Edward, 79
Henley, Robert, 23
Herring's Mill, 15
Hesketh Crescent, 20, 44, 45, 46, 47, 48, 49, 50, 52, 53, 54, 65, 67, 135
Higher Terrace, 5, 22, 124, 126, 127, 128, 135
Hockings Farm, 77, 78
Hockings, John, 77
Hope's Nose, 26, 50, 65
Hutchings, Mrs, 126

Ilsham Valley, 56, 60
Inner Harbour, 26, 123, 125, 127, 128, 131, 133, 137, 139
Judas Tree, 88
Kent's Cavern, 1, 2, 19, 20
Kenton, 6
Keyse, Emma, 68
Kilmorie, 20, 47, 50
King, Colin, 64
King, Fred, 64
King George VI, 136
King's Drive, 8, 10, 26
King's Gardens, 14, 26
Kingskerswell, 12, 21, 23
Knolls Quarry, 54
Lang, George, 29
Langmead, Samuel, 81
Lavender Cottage, 84, 85
Lea Cottage, 82, 83, 84
Lee, John, 68
Lime Avenue, 8
Lipscombe, Edwin, 132
Livermead, 10, 22, 45, 139
Living Coasts, 123, 137, 138, 141, 144
Long Avenue, 8
Long Quarry, 66, 98
Lucius Street, 8
Lummaton Quarry, 77, 78, 104
MacEnery, Father John, 19
Maddock, Miss Hilda, 86
Maidencombe, 17, 18, 66, 67, 87, 88, 89, 90, 91
Mallard, William B, 29
Mallock Clock Tower, 3, 5, 122, 124
Mallock, Richard, 124
Marchetti, Joseph, 126

Marine Spa, 123, 136, 137, 140, 141
Marldon, 12
Meadfoot, 1, 10, 44, 50, 52, 55, 65
Meadfoot Beach, 20, 44, 45, 46, 48, 49, 50, 51, 52, 54, 55, 56, 65, 135
Medical Baths, 135
Millennium Bridge, 122, 132, 133, 137, 142
Mojo Cafe Bar, 40,
Montague, Jessy, 25
Moran, John, 136, 140,
Morrison, Sir James, 20, 25, 68, 96
Moxhay, Richard 18, 76
Musical fete champetre, 17, 91, 92, 93
Napoleonic Wars, 124
National Coastwatch Institute, 44, 55, 56, 62, 64, 65
National Home Guard Memorial, 11
Newfoundland, 124
North Pier, 125, 132, 133, 139
Nostra Senora del Rosario, 9
Oddicombe Beach, 66, 95, 96, 97, 98, 99
Ogilvie, Arthur, 19
Old Maid's Perch, 10, 23, 26, 28, 31, 35, 36, 38, 40, 41, 42
Old Manor House, 85, 103
Old Mill Road, 8, 13, 14, 15, 16
Orestone, 20, 48, 54
Osborne Hotel, 20, 47, 48, 50
Palk, Robert, 125
Palk, Sir Lawrence, 124, 125, 127, 128, 139
Palk, Sir Lawrence H, 19
Palk, Sir Lawrence V, 45,

Palm Court Hotel, 7, 10, 22, 30, 31, 32, 36, 37, 38, 39, 40, 41, 42
Park Crescent, 75, 76
Pavilion, 26, 50, 122, 125, 129, 130, 131, 132, 142, 144
Peaked Tor Cove, 137
Pearce, Nathaniel, 81
Penney's Cottage, 105, 109, 110, 111, 112
Petheridge, James, 75
Petit Tor Beach, 93, 94, 95
Phillimore, Rear-Admiral Augustus, 62
Pitts, Thomas, 81
Pixies, 19
Pollard, Dr, 133, 138, 139
Pomery Bridge, 14, 15
Powe, Francis, 19
Prince Albert, 66, 67, 70, 71, 94
Princess Gardens, 6, 10, 130
Princess Theatre, 7, 23, 33 142
Proserpine, 58, 59, 60, 61, 62
Prospect Cottage, 80, 85
Queen Victoria, 3, 5, 67, 70, 71, 124
Queen's Hotel, 3, 4, 126
RAF, 36, 135
Raleigh, Sir Walter, 6, 9
Regina Hotel, 124, 133, 134, 135, 142
River Fleete, 16, 77, 103, 104, 105, 106, 107, 108, 110, 111, 112, 113, 114, 115, 116, 117, 118, 119, 125, 127, 128
RNLI, 62
Rock Cottage, 7, 29
Rock End Mansion, 44, 57
Rock House, 129

Rock Walk, 6, 10, 22, 25, 27, 28, 31, 32, 37, 50, 142
Rose Cottage Tea Rooms, 12
Royal Hotel, 5, 123, 126, 127
Royal Terrace Gardens, 28
Royal Torbay Yacht Club, 65, 136
Ruiter, Admiral, 121
St Augustine's Church, 84, 85
St John's Church, 22, 52, 94, 128, 142
St Mary Magdalene Church, 114
St Marychurch, 3, 5, 6, 12, 18, 19, 30, 66, 67, 68, 69, 71, 72, 73, 74, 75, 77, 79, 81, 87, 88, 93, 94, 101, 102, 121, 124
Sands Lane, 8
Shag Rock, 20, 48, 54
Sheddon Hill, 10, 23, 25, 36, 39
Sherwell Stream, 14, 15
Sherwell Valley Road, 14
South Pier, 122, 126, 133, 142
Spanish Barn, 9, 10
Splatt, William Francis, 4
Staddon, James, 81
Stokes, Jeff and Lucy, 99, 100
Stoney Combe, 109
Strand, 2, 3, 5, 10, 122, 123, 124, 125, 126
Sulyarde Terrace, 6, 22
Sykes, Eric, 131
Tanner family, 136
Tayleur, Charles, 69
Taylor, Samuel Henley, 81
Terry, John, 81
Thatched Tavern, 87, 88
Thatcher Rock, 20, 48, 54
The Bath House, 133, 134, 138, 139
The Bath Saloons, 138, 139, 141

The Demon Hunter, 20, 44, 53, 58, 59, 60, 62
The White House, 5
Toll House, 7, 10, 25, 29, 32, 33, 34, 38, 43
Tollemache, Mr, 68
Toms, John, 81
Tor Hill Cottages, 84, 85
Torabbey Park, 8
Torbay Council, 10, 12, 16, 26, 41, 42, 50, 52, 79, 87, 118, 136, 143
Torbay Hotel, 6, 10, 22, 129
Torbay Royal Regatta, 136
Torquay Boys' Grammar School, 4
Torquay Harbour, 16, 17, 22, 23, 24, 44, 55, 56, 64, 65, 71, 79, 80, 91, 94, 107, 118, 119, 121, 140, 144
Torquay Museum, 1, 2, 12, 19, 114, 132, 129
Torquay Station, 3, 5, 29
Torquay Town Hall, 4, 77, 113
Torquay Volunteer Company, 11
Torre Abbey, 1, 7, 8, 9, 10, 14, 19, 23, 26, 28, 117, 124, 142
Torre Abbey Meadows, 7, 10, 14, 23, 24
Torre Abbey Sands, 24, 26, 31, 34, 36, 38, 39, 50, 142
Torre Church, 8, 79
Torwood Gardens, 2
Trams, 29, 30, 31, 32
Triangle Point, 48, 51, 54
Troward, Charles, 80, 81
Union Hotel, 114
Union Street, 3, 16, 105, 108, 114, 115, 119

Upton, 1, 16, 17, 80, 108, 111, 113, 119, 121, 142
Upton Park, 113
US 4th Infantry Division, 143, 144
Valley of the Rocks, 17, 90, 91, 92, 93, 101
Vane Hill, 123, 126
Vaughan Parade, 117, 122, 125, 127, 128, 129, 133
Vaughan Terrace, 126, 127, 128, 135, 142
Victoria Parade, 3, 122, 123, 125, 126
Vincent, Carole, 129
Vivian, Edward, 11
Walling, James, 81
Wall's Hill, 55, 96, 98, 99
Watcombe, 1, 16, 17, 18, 66, 67, 73, 77, 87, 90, 91, 92, 101, 103, 104, 119
Wesleyan Chapel, 79, 128
Wesleyan Church, 2
William's Field, 106
Wills, William, 81
Windmill Hill, 109
Woodley, Mr, 71, 72, 93, 94
Worth, Harry, 131
Wyatt, Mary, 129

Printed in Poland
by Amazon Fulfillment
Poland Sp. z o.o., Wrocław